BIBLE
Comes to Life

Book 1
CREATION

Joy Sukadi | Lilyana Margaretha

BIBLE COMES TO LIFE

BOOK 1: CREATION (REVISED EDITION)

© 2021 by Joy Sukadi and Lilyana Margaretha

All rights reserved. No part of this book may be reproduced, stored in a retrieval system, or transmitted in any form or by any means — electronic, mechanical, digital, photocopy, recording, or any other — except for brief quotations in printed reviews, without prior written permission from the publisher.

Unless otherwise indicated, all Scripture quotations are taken from the Holy Bible, New Living Translation, copyright © 1996, 2004, 2015 by Tyndale House Foundation. Used by permission of Tyndale House Publishers, Inc., Carol Stream, Illinois 60188. All rights reserved.

Scripture quotations marked NIV are taken from the Holy Bible, New International Version®, NIV®. Copyright © 1973, 1978, 1984, 2011 by Biblica, Inc.® Used by permission. All rights reserved worldwide.

Scripture quotations marked ESV are taken from the Holy Bible, English Standard Version® (ESV®). Copyright © 2001 by Crossway, a publishing ministry of Good News Publishers. All rights reserved. ESV Text Edition: 2016.

Scripture quotations marked MSG are taken from the Holy Bible, The Message. Copyright © 1993, 2002, 2018 by Eugene H. Peterson.

Scripture quotations marked NIrV are taken from the Holy Bible, New International Reader's Version®, NIrV®. Copyright © 1995, 1996, 1998, 2014 by Biblica, Inc.® Used by permission of Zondervan. All rights reserved worldwide. www.zondervan.com. The "NIrV" and "New International Reader's Version" are trademarks registered in the United States Patent and Trademark Office by Biblica, INC.™

All emphasis in Scripture has been added.

Editor: Pam Lagomarsino

Illustrations: Natalia Wijaya and Joy Sukadi

Interior and Cover Design: Samuel Sutanto

Cover Image: Guy Megides

A list of photo/image credits is at the end of this book.

ISBN: 978-1-7376802-4-6

Published by Sharpening Little Arrows, LLC
Mill Creek, WA 98012
www.sharpeninglittlearrows.com
E-mail: sharpeninglittlearrows@gmail.com

Welcome to Bible Comes to Life!....................................5

Introduction..10

Quick Start Guide..11

Material List...12

1-1: Theory Buster: The Big Bang.............................15

1-2: Theory Buster: The Random Chance 27

1-3: Theory Buster: Evolution 41

1-4: Theory Buster: We're Relatives with Chimps!...53

1-5: Dinosaurs and Dragons 65

1-6: Where Did All the Dinosaurs Go?.....................79

1-7: God Made Boys and Girls.................................93

1-8: Living on Purpose..107

1-9: God's Unique Masterpiece..............................119

1-10: You Are Chosen!..135

Truth Blast!..150

Notes...154

Photo Credits..160

Welcome to Bible Comes to Life!

"Equipping Children with Biblical Truths to Challenge Cultural Lies"

DEAR FRIENDS,

Our journey started in 2019 as our children were elementary school age. We observed the world around us and noticed we are raising our children in a different day and age now. They are bombarded daily with a progressive agenda, lies, perversity, and skewed truth through media, school indoctrination, perverse library books, and more. This simple question filled our hearts: How do we equip our children to stand strong against popular beliefs and cultural lies? The current is strong; the pressure is great. We heard so many stories of kids with Christian upbringing turn away from their faith once they go to college (or even earlier!).

During that discouraging time, God spoke clearly in our hearts: **"Daughters, you cannot stop the flood from coming, but you can start building an ark for your family—intentionally and with a purpose. Your family will be saved!"** We could not stop the nonbiblical culture from bombarding our children, but we could win this battle by equipping them from the inside out! In this saturated "woke" culture, sending our children to Sunday schools, youth groups, or summer Bible camps will not be enough anymore. Discipleship and equipping need to happen every day, in our homes, by the closest people raising them—*us!* The Word of God in Psalm 127:4 (NIV) resonated loud and clear in our hearts:

> *"Like arrows in the hands of a warrior are children born in one's youth."*

As parents, we are called to shape our next generation so they can be as sharp as arrows. We are assigned to raise sons and daughters of clarity who can detect the enemy's lies from hundreds of miles away. We must equip them daily with biblical truths so they can push back the darkness and defend the truth. The Bible tells us in 1 Peter 3:15:

> "Instead, you must worship Christ as Lord of your life. And if someone asks about your hope as a believer, always be ready to explain it."

In creating this "Bible Comes to Life" series, we hope and pray we will equip our children in a logical way so they can boldly defend their faith as they grow up. Here you will find resources to do intentional discipleship in the heart of your homes. This series will help you instill biblical values and teach solid apologetic truths to your children in **relevant and engaging** ways. The best part of all: we use SCIENCE and logical explanations to support the biblical truth. We know children are highly visual with short attention spans. Their curious minds respond best to *exciting games, science experiments, arts and crafts, and compelling story-telling from their parents.* Even Jesus talks in parables.

With constant streams of games and entertainment surrounding our children, the Bible could become an archaic and irrelevant resource for them if we are not careful. Our vision is to bring the Bible to life again in our children's hearts by presenting God's Word in the most exciting, creative ways. We want kids to experience, taste, and see how real and magnificent our Creator is.

We designed this book series **for busy families** like yours and mine. It is filled with **fundamental biblical values to impart**. In each lesson, we compare a non-biblical worldview and a biblical worldview. We then support the biblical values with an *activity, experiment, arts and crafts, or other methods* to make the Bible relevant. The activities are so simple that you can find materials in your kitchen or a short trip to the craft store. Each lesson will take about thirty to forty-five minutes. Lessons can also promote fun family time on the weekends, during summer vacation when children are not in school, or even during the busiest weeknights!

Finally, at the end of each lesson, you will find intriguing questions to foster a meaningful family discussion. This time provides opportunities for you, parents, to open up about your past, tell heartfelt stories, and "download" unforgettable truths into your children's hearts. It basically kills two birds with one stone: **creating a strong bond within your family while also building a solid biblical foundation in your children's lives.** See this book as your eternal investment to launch your children into the world prepared and ready to defend their Christian faith. We are excited to be on this journey with you!

For our children's souls,
Joy and Lilyana

> The training of children in the fundamental doctrines of the Christian faith is essential for the Church to continue from generation to generation. In order for this training to be effective, it needs to incorporate several key ingredients: **exposure to what the Bible says, a clear connection between that and the real world, realistic ways for children to understand complex concepts and suggestions for parents to reinforce the ideas at home with their children.** The *Bible Comes to Life,* Book 1 on *Creation* incorporates all of these in a quality book that children will enjoy as they discover things about themselves and the world around them. It is an attractive resource for teachers and parents to make the biblical teaching exciting to learn.
>
> **Lanny Hubbard**
> *Professor of Theology, Portland Bible College*

Book 1

Creation

In the beginning God created the heavens and the earth.

Genesis 1:1

Introduction

Many parents have a "wait-and-see" approach. We often wait until our children are older to understand the Bible. We wait until they really need some corrections and life-changing lessons. We wait until we are equipped with more knowledge. We wait and wait … until it's becoming too late.

In reality, everything we need to teach our children about God's truth is already there in front of our eyes. God, the Initiator, has laid the foundation for us. The Bible is filled with His truth, promises, signs, wonders, directions, and purpose. Our job as parents is to partner with Him in teaching our children.

> Are we willing to respond to God's calling to intentionally plant God's truths in our little ones' precious hearts?

Where do we even start? There is no right or wrong answer to this question. However, we would love to start our journey from the book of Genesis. If our children cannot trust the beginning of the Bible, they will have a hard time believing the rest of it!

Through the lessons in this book, we will learn about God who created everything and saw that it was *very* good. He is a **God of order and purpose**. His creation work is just beyond words, too big to understand with our limited human mind. These lessons will show and prove the work of an Intelligent Designer. We are here not just by a random chance or coincidence.

Not only is our God a majestic Creator, but He is also a personal God who desires to connect with us every day. As we look at all the evidence and truths surrounding the book of Genesis, we will gain insights into our true identity and who we are in Him. We are designed in His image, full of glorious purpose, fearfully and wonderfully made. Let's begin!

Quick Start Guide

We know you are eager to jump into the lessons. But before you do, here are a few important things to note.

Each chapter contains a lesson ready to be read aloud by the parent(s). In each lesson, you will find:

- Purpose
- Icebreaker (either questions, a mini-game, or a short story)
- Introduction
- Non-biblical View
- Biblical View
- Activity (including materials and instructions): science experiments, engineering, games, arts and crafts, or cooking.
- Discussion
- Summary
- Truth to Remember
- Memory Verse
- Fact Check (in some lessons)

The instructions in the **Activity** sections are a guideline for parents. Although you will find most materials easily in your house, we recommend checking the Activity section at least a few days before the lesson to prepare the materials. Some activities may need a simple preparation that takes more than one day (for those few, we noted that at the end of the preceding lesson).

The **Discussion** section has expected answers in parentheses for questions that need definite answers. Some questions also have additional read-aloud parts to solidify the truths and make connections after children give their answers.

At the end of some lessons is a **Fact Check** section for parents and older children to dig deeper into the Scripture, scientific and historical facts, famous people's quotes, or other resources.

At the end of this book, you will find the **"Truth Blast!"** section. Here, we compiled a list of Truths and key Bible verses from all the lessons. Check out this section as you go along in the lessons to see how each lesson ties into the big picture and for a quick reference in the future.

Last but not least, find extra resources (links to videos and articles) at our website: **www.sharpeninglittlearrows.com**

Material List

As promised, we want to make it as easy as possible for you to use this book. So, we put together a list of all materials you will need in the lessons for your quick reference.

1-1 COLORED SODA ERUPTION

- Four small bottles of unopened clear soda (for example, Sprite)
- Mentos chewy mints (any flavors)
- Four colors of kids paints or food coloring
- Baking tray or any container
- Thick paper

1-2 PUZZLE JACKPOT

- A simple jigsaw puzzle with at least ten pieces (If you don't have a puzzle, ten LEGO bricks and mini-figures will work as well.)
- Paper
- Pencil

1-3 LEGO MASTERS CHAMPIONSHIP

- LEGO bricks
- Colored pencils
- Paper

1-4 DNA ALPHABET

- Materials with four different colors (at least twenty pieces of each color). Choose one from the following list: building blocks of similar size, beads, pom poms, colorful cereals (such as Fruit Loops), or candies.
- String or pipe cleaners (optional—if using beads or cereals)

1-5 DIGGING DINOSAUR FOSSILS

Note: Prepare for the activity at least one and a half hours before the lesson.

- Two cups of cornstarch
- One cup of water
- Medium-sized oven-safe container
- Dinosaur toy figures
- Other small materials, such as rocks or gems (optional)
- Digging tools, such as toy hammers, toothbrushes, paintbrushes, plastic knives, or other tools safe for kids.
- Old newspaper or tray (optional)

1-6 THREE-LAYERED FOSSIL ICE BLOCK

Note: Prepare for the activity at least two days before the lesson.

- A tall plastic container (at least five inches high with a wide opening)
- Three different colors of food coloring
- Animal toy figures (or small flat stones and markers or acrylic paints)
- Digging tools, such as toy hammers, spoons, or any other tools safe for children
- A large tray or baking dish
- Warm water in squirt bottles or cups (optional)
- Salt (optional)
- Three pieces of paper

1-7 FORK AND SPOON CHALLENGE

- Forks and spoons
- One pack of instant noodles per family member
- Two bowls for each person
- A timer
- A tray or cookie sheet for each person (optional)

1-8 THE SUN AND THE MOON

- A small mirror
- A flashlight
- A stack of books (optional)

1-9 FINGERPRINTING

- Pencil
- Light-colored paper
- Clear tape
- Magnifying glass (optional)

1-10 CONSTELLATION JARS

Note: The following list is for one constellation jar. Your family can make one constellation jar for the whole family or one for each family member.

- A glass jar (wide enough to fit a small light inside)—*for each constellation jar*
- A piece of light-colored construction paper —*for each constellation jar*
- Aluminum foil
- Ruler
- String or yarn
- Scissors
- Tape
- Pushpins or bamboo skewers (or any sharp objects to poke holes)
- A piece of cardboard (optional)
- Pen or marker
- Battery-operated light, such as tea light, LED click light, or string light—*for each constellation jar*

1-1

Theory Buster: The Big Bang

1-1 Theory Buster: The Big Bang

PURPOSE

To investigate the beginning of the universe: Did it explode out of nowhere, or was there a cause behind its origin?

Icebreaker

- Suppose you come home from school and find a beautiful, wrapped present at the dining table with your name on it. What would be the first thing that comes into your mind?

- Would you think this beautiful present just came out of nowhere, or would you wonder who gave it to you?

Have you ever gazed at the moon and stars on a clear night? Do you like to take a walk in nature, discovering new critters and enjoying the colorful flowers? In nature, we see some parts of the huge universe.

> *"The Universe is everything we can touch, feel, sense, measure or detect. It includes living things, planets, stars, galaxies, dust clouds, light, and even time. Before the birth of the Universe, time, space, and matter did not exist."[1]*

So, how did all these things start? Today, we will explore together how the universe was formed.

• • •

NON-BIBLICAL VIEW

What do our science books or teachers tell us about how the universe was formed? Today, most scientists and people who study the stars believe in the "Big Bang Theory."[2] They tell us how the universe started from a clump of matter packed very tightly into a small space—even smaller than the top of a little pin! Then *suddenly*, it exploded with a powerful blast, and the universe got bigger and colder. Scientists think that teeny, tiny parts of light filled the universe at that moment.

But, there are still some things they don't understand even today:

Where did the matter come from?

What caused the sudden "Big Bang" explosion of light and energy?

Many believe the Big Bang just happened for *no reason*, and no creator made it happen. Did this universe really just explode out of nowhere?

BIBLICAL VIEW

Let's look at Genesis 1:1–3:

> *In the beginning God created the heavens and the earth. The earth was formless and empty, and darkness covered the deep waters. And the Spirit of God was hovering over the surface of the waters. Then God said, "Let there be light," and there was light.*

The Bible says God was the Creator of the universe, and He made the light that filled the universe. In other words, God is the *cause** of the universe. The universe did not just explode out of nowhere and for no reason.

Is it true there must be a cause for something to happen? Let's do an experiment together!

---

*A **cause** is something or someone that makes things happen.

1-1 Theory Buster: The Big Bang

Activity

Colored Soda Eruption

MATERIALS

- Four small unopened clear soda bottles (for example, Sprite). Use newly-opened soda. Flat soda will NOT make any foamy eruption.
- Mentos chewy mints (any flavors)
- Four colors of kids paints or food coloring
- Baking tray or any container (to contain the eruption and catch the mess)
- Thick paper (to capture the colored eruption to create a painting)

Note: A simpler alternative is the classic Coke and Mentos experiment to create a foamy eruption.

1-1 Theory Buster: The Big Bang

INSTRUCTIONS

1. Put each soda bottle on top of a piece of paper. Use a baking tray or any container underneath for easier clean-up.

2. Open the soda bottles one by one. Carefully squirt in about a tablespoon of paint or food coloring into each soda bottle—one color for each bottle. Do not stir.
3. Quickly put a Mentos candy into each soda bottle.
4. Watch as the colored eruption begins.

1-1 Theory Buster: The Big Bang

Hang the painting to dry and enjoy your new masterpiece!

Discussion

1. Let's talk about "the surprise present" introduced earlier. Do you think this present came out of nowhere? Or did it have a cause? What is the cause of the surprise present?

   *(**Answer:** Someone must have carefully wrapped and given you that gift. That present did not just suddenly appear out of nowhere.)*

   So, everything that comes into existence must have a cause.

   (Look at the "Kalam cosmological argument" in the Fact Check section for more details.)

2. In our experiment today, do you think the soda could just explode out of nowhere? Which step did we need to make the eruption start? In other words, what is the *cause* of the eruption?

   *(**Answer:** Someone putting a Mentos candy in the soda bottle is the cause.)*

3. What kind of cause could have started the universe? Think of a word to describe this cause.

1-1 Theory Buster: The Big Bang

4. Is there anything in the Big Bang theory that is similar to what the Bible says about how the universe began?

   _____
   _____
   _____

   (Answer: The details about how it happened might be different. But both agree the universe was suddenly born in a flash of light in the past.)

5. What is the main difference between the Big Bang theory and the story of creation in Genesis 1? Which truth makes more sense and could have happened: an explosion without a cause (blowing up out of nowhere) or a universe formed by Someone powerful and creative?

   _____
   _____
   _____

6. What would you say to your friends if they disagree with you about how the world was created?

   _____
   _____
   _____

   (Discuss how the children should respond if they hear or read about the Big Bang theory in school or anywhere else.)

Summary

Everything that happens and has a beginning must have a cause. The universe did not just explode out of nowhere for no reason, like in the Big Bang theory. God is the cause of the beginning of our universe and everything else in it.

1-1 Theory Buster: The Big Bang

Truth to Remember

God is *the cause* of the beginning of the universe.

He made heaven and earth,
the sea, and everything in them.
He keeps every promise forever.

Psalm 146:6

FACT CHECK

COSMOLOGY:
The study of how the universe began

KALAM COSMOLOGICAL ARGUMENT:
1. Everything that has a beginning has a cause.
2. The universe has a beginning.
3. So the universe has a cause.

The Muslim scholars who lived many centuries ago used this argument to explain how the universe began. It was then used and popularized by an American philosopher and Christian scholar, William Lane Craig, in his book in 1979.[3] Dr. Craig explained the cause of the universe has to be personal and timeless—and the only possible cause that meets these criteria is God.[4,5]

THE SCIENCE BEHIND THE "MENTOS AND SODA" EXPERIMENT:

The foamy eruption that happens as we drop Mentos candies into soda is a physical reaction called "bubble nucleation."

When we open a fresh soda bottle, we would hear a whooshing sound from CO_2 gas escaping. Then bubbles form and float to the top of the soda. This usually happens slowly because the water in the soda helps trap the gas in place.

When we drop Mentos candies into soda, this reaction happens rapidly because the candy surface has a lot of tiny bumps. Numerous little bubbles of CO_2 will form on the rough candy surface. This bubble nucleation process breaks the bonds between CO_2 and the water more quickly, resulting in a towering foam geyser.

1-2

Theory Buster:
The Random Chance

1-2 Theory Buster: The Random Chance

PURPOSE
To investigate whether life on Earth happens by *random chance* or *finely tuned* by an Intelligent Designer.

Icebreaker

- Imagine you were stranded on an island, away from everybody and all by yourself. Which three items would you like to have with you?

- With those three items, how long do you think you could survive?

Do you remember what we learned about the start of the universe? Yes, God is the *cause* of the beginning of the universe. Today, let's ask some questions:

- How can humans, plants, animals, and other tiny living things live and survive in the universe?
- Did it just happen randomly?
- Or is there an intelligent mind who made "just the right" place and things for us to have life?

Before we answer these questions, let's look at what makes a place good enough to live in.

• • •

Do you remember the story of Goldilocks and the three bears? She was looking for *just the right* chair, bowl of porridge, and bed in the bears' house. She would not settle for things that were too big, too small, too hot, or too cold.

Goldilocks wasn't the only one who needed something just right. A scientist at NASA said for a place to have life, it needs to have two things:

1. Water and the right temperature (if it's too cold, the water will freeze; if it's too hot, the water will evaporate and "disappear")
2. Energy sources.[1]

Can you guess which planet has those? You're right! Earth is the only planet we know of to have the liquid water that life needs.

1-2 Theory Buster: The Random Chance

Scientists agree that how far away Earth is from the sun is just right. Earth is in a "habitable zone"—a place that can have life in it. If Earth was too close to the sun, the water would evaporate, which means to turn from a liquid to a gas. If it was too far from the sun, Earth would turn into a frozen snowball.

Another scientist said living creatures need many other things to survive in this universe.[2] He said each thing has to be exact and carefully adjusted (or finely tuned) to make it just right. So, we need the right size of a planet, the right amount of gravity*, and a special layer around the planet called the atmosphere to protect it from harmful burning from the sun. These are just a few examples. Another scientist, listed **140 different things life needs** to exist in the universe![3]

If Goldilocks were to find a just-right planet to live in, what planet do you think she would choose?

You are correct! Our planet Earth is not too hot, too cold, too big, or too small. Do you know Earth is "the Goldilocks Planet"? Why? Because Earth is the only planet in our solar system that is *just right* for life to happen! It has all the right things to make it livable.

***Gravity** is a powerful pull to make things come toward other things—like dropping a ball and it pulls to the ground.

NON-BIBLICAL VIEW

However, many scientists believe Earth has all the right things by *random chance* or *coincidence*. In other words, they think Earth is just "lucky" to have all the right settings happening in one place.

But, is it possible to have all 140 different things—"just right" in one place—if it's only by chance?

BIBLICAL VIEW

The Bible says, "In the beginning God created the heavens and the earth" (Genesis 1:1). On the first day of creation, God made the Earth. Not only did God create Earth, but He also kept doing His creation work for six days in a row: making the light, separating the water from the land, creating the sun, moon, and stars, and filling Earth with different forms of life. He was very busy!

God made sure everything was in place just right to support life on Earth.

So, how do we explain life on Earth as the only "Goldilocks planet" we know about? Did all the right things happen randomly *by chance*? Or is there a *Creator* who planned and carefully placed everything together for life to exist? Let's do an experiment about "random chance" to help us understand better.

1-2 Theory Buster: The Random Chance

Activity
Puzzle Jackpot

MATERIALS

- A simple jigsaw puzzle (with at least ten pieces)

Alternative materials

If you don't have a puzzle, ten LEGO bricks and minifigures will work as well. Instead of throwing puzzle pieces, throw LEGO bricks and minifigures to see whether they can land perfectly to "just the right" placement.

- 10 pieces of jigsaw puzzle

1-2 Theory Buster: The Random Chance

INSTRUCTIONS

1. Find and put together ten adjacent puzzle pieces to see what it should look like. If you use ten LEGO bricks and minifigures, determine what they should look like as a reference. (For example, three minifigures standing in the center, four red bricks on the left, and three green bricks on the right.)

2. Take a picture of these ten puzzle or LEGO pieces together as a reference for the "just right" position.

3. Ask a family member to take two adjacent pieces from the ten-piece puzzle or LEGO bricks and throw them in the air. Compare the landing position to the reference. Say:

> "Let's see how many times you can make these two pieces land perfectly next to each other."

(No matter how many times you throw the puzzle or LEGO pieces, it will be difficult to have them coincidentally fall into the right spots.)

1-2 Theory Buster: The Random Chance

4. Have another family member do the same thing with three puzzle or LEGO pieces.

5. Go around the table and throw increasing numbers of puzzle or LEGO pieces into the air. You may stop the experiment *anytime* once your children realize **it's nearly impossible to align the pieces correctly with random throws.**

Discussion

1. What do you think of our experiment today?

2. With more puzzle or LEGO pieces, is it easier or harder to make them land perfectly? What are the chances of throwing 10 pieces in the air and they fit perfectly when they land? How about 20 pieces? 30 pieces? 140 pieces? Will it ever be possible?

3. Let's say each puzzle or LEGO piece is one thing life needs in the universe, such as gravity, temperature, and many others. Remember, a scientist made a list of 140 different things for life to exist, so it is like having 140 pieces fitting perfectly in one place. Would it be possible for *all* of the right things to happen in one place randomly?

1-2 Theory Buster: The Random Chance

4. Let's use gravity as an example. Gravity is one thing a place needs to make it fit to live in, just like this puzzle piece *(hold a puzzle piece)*. Is it important to have the right amount of gravity where we live? Why do you think so?

Imagine standing on Jupiter, the largest planet in our solar system. The surface of Jupiter is not firm like Earth's; it's made of gases. Jupiter's gravity is bigger than Earth's. If you could stand on Jupiter, it would be like having something very heavy glued to your legs. And of course, you would quickly sink into the planet![4]

Or imagine living in a place with less or no gravity. Can you picture yourself floating around like the astronauts living in outer space? Not just for days or months, but all your life. Simple tasks like eating, sleeping, taking a shower, and using the toilet would be really hard!

We need just the right amount of gravity to have life on Earth as we do today.

5. Let's take a vote today. Which one sounds more likely: all the right things on Earth happened on their own (by random chance), or a Creator planned and carefully adjusted *everything* to make life on Earth possible?

Summary

For living things to live and survive in a certain place, many different things have to be finely tuned. They cannot happen by random chance. God is the Intelligent Designer who makes Earth "the Goldilocks planet"—the only planet with just the right things for life to happen.

1-2 Theory Buster: The Random Chance

Truth to Remember

Life on Earth is possible because God finely tuned it to make it just right.

God created everything through him, and nothing was created except through him.

John 1:3

1-2 Theory Buster: The Random Chance

FACT CHECK

DID YOU KNOW?

Earth's size is just right to make life possible.

If Earth were larger, the gravity pull would be greater. The atmosphere (the protective layer around the planet) would keep other gases (Hydrogen and Helium), making this layer too heavy. Earth would become too hot for liquid water to exist.

If Earth were smaller, it would not be able to keep a warm enough atmosphere. The interior of Earth would cool rapidly. Earth would lose the magnetic field needed to maintain the atmosphere.

HOW ABOUT PLANET MARS?

Although Mars is almost within the sun's habitable zone, it is too small.

Mars is like a frozen desert with a thin atmosphere, solidified interior, and virtually no magnetic field.[5]

1-3

Theory Buster: Evolution

1-3 Theory Buster: Evolution

PURPOSE
To investigate whether the theory of evolution through natural selection is true.

Icebreaker

- What is the most amazing creation you've ever made? (It could be a cake you baked, a LEGO creation you built, or even the last snowman you made together with your family.)
- Was it hard to make? How many hours did you spend completing it?
- Imagine you don't have to do anything, and the things you need to make your cake (such as eggs, flour, and sugar) can change slowly into a yummy cake on their own. Or imagine your loose LEGO bricks suddenly turn into a cool LEGO creation without you helping or doing anything. Can these happen?

1-3 Theory Buster: Evolution

We learned God is the Creator of the universe, and He made life possible on Earth. Today, we will learn more and zoom in on how living things (plants, animals, and human beings) came to life.

Even though scientists know about millions of insects, animals, and plants living on Earth, there are still a lot more that remain a complete mystery.[1]

How did so many different types of animals and plants come to life?

Most people believe in one of the two theories: **evolution** or **creation**. (Evolution might seem like a big word to some of us. It simply means changing slowly from a simple thing, like a bag of flour, to a more complex form, like a beautiful yummy cake.)

• • •

NON-BIBLICAL VIEW

Many scientists believe our world began *billions of years* ago, and living things came from non-living things (but they don't know how this happened!).

In 1859, a scientist named Charles Darwin wrote about an idea in his book *The Origin of Species*.[2] Mr. Darwin thought living things started from a simple, one-celled life form, like the amoeba here. It is very tiny, lives in water, and can only be seen under a microscope. *(See the picture of amoeba.)*

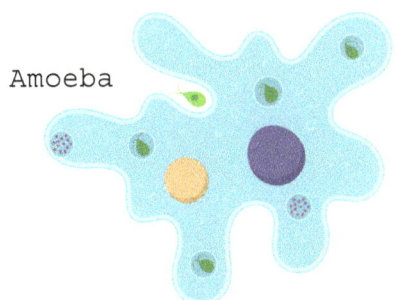
Amoeba

This simple life form then changed over millions of years into more complex animals.[3] This process is called "evolution." Mr. Darwin's idea became famous all over the world, and people know it as the "evolution theory."

43

1-3 Theory Buster: Evolution

(If you haven't heard of Mr. Darwin's theory before, most likely you will find it later in science books, school textbooks, movies, museums, or other places.)

Theory of Evolution

Scientists like Mr. Darwin believe one kind of animal can "evolve" (or change slowly) into a different kind of animal.[4]

Here's a short story of animal evolution. Clap or jump every time you hear the word "**evolved**," and try counting how many times you hear this word (**Hint:** Whenever you hear the word "**evolved**," it means an animal changes to a totally different kind of animal over millions of years.).

> *Hundreds of millions of years ago, a certain type of fish **evolved** into amphibians (animals that can live both in water and on land, like frogs and toads). The amphibians then **evolved** into reptiles (animals that live on land only, like crocodiles, snakes, and turtles). Some types of reptiles then **evolved** into mammals (like apes and monkeys), and birds. Finally, certain mammals **evolved** into human beings.*

How many times did you hear the word "evolved"?
(***Answer***: *four times*)

BIBLICAL VIEW

The Bible, instead, points to a creation theory: a Creator made the world and everything in it—the plants, reptiles, fish, elephants … basically every living thing you can name! (Genesis 1-2, Psalm 146:6). This creation work is an "intelligent design"— a brilliant work by a smart and creative mind.

People who believe in the creation theory think more complex creatures can never evolve from simpler forms on their own. In other words, a fish can never turn into a monkey.

> This whole universe is so complex. It must have been planned by an "intelligent being."

Just like our cake and LEGO masterpiece, they need **us** as intelligent beings to create something spectacular.

People who believe in evolution argue creation or intelligent design is not real. No scientific evidence can ever prove it! They think it's just a religious idea, not a scientific fact. But, real explanations and proof show the creation theory is true. We will dive into the "intelligent design" idea through our activity today.

1-3 Theory Buster: Evolution

Activity

LEGO Masters Championship

MATERIALS

- LEGO bricks
- Colored pencils
- Paper

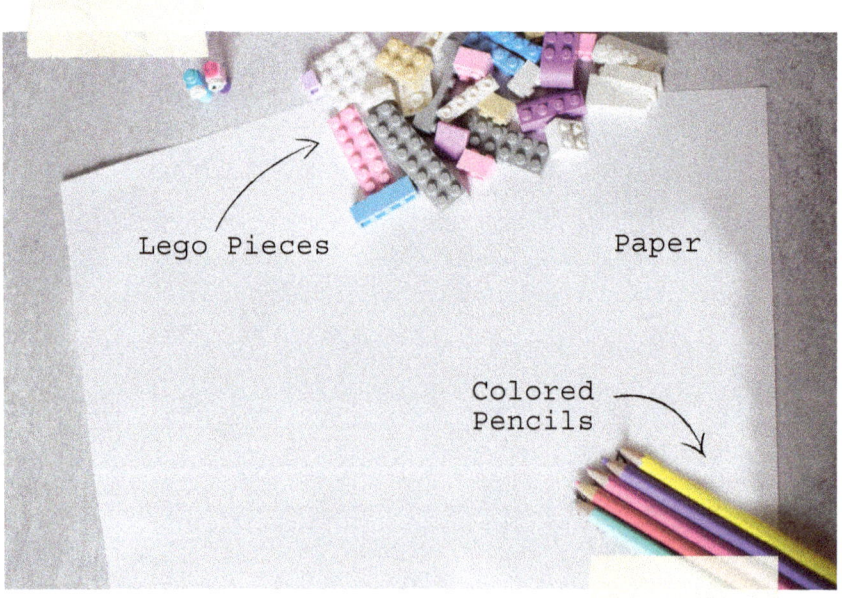

INSTRUCTIONS

1. Give a piece of paper and colored pencils to each family member.
2. The challenge is to design a creation using the LEGO bricks. Decide the theme of this competition (for example, the most modern-looking robot, the comfiest vacation home with swimming pools, etc.).

3. Set a timer (thirty to sixty minutes) to sketch ideas on paper and build the LEGO masterpiece.

4. After the time is up, let family members explain their designs and present their creations.
5. Declare the winners for the following criteria: the best overall design, the most "out-of-the-box" creation, and the best color coordination.

1-3 Theory Buster: Evolution

Discussion

1. If we leave the loose LEGO bricks here for a super long time (let's say for a million years), will they ever "evolve" into a bigger creation, like these robots or houses? Or will the LEGO bricks stay the same? After a long time, will their shapes and colors become better or worse?

2. Do you remember the last time you made a snowman with your family? Is it possible for the snowflakes falling from the sky to "evolve" into snowmen if we don't design and build them?

```
"Don't be silly!
Nobody made me.
I evolved slowly.
from snowflakes!"
- Mr. Snowman
```

3. The evolution theory suggests creations like human beings evolved from one-celled life forms, fish, amphibians, reptiles, and other mammals. What do you think of this theory? Does it make more sense if we are created by a higher intelligent being like God?

4. The evolution theory says animals evolved by "natural selection" or survival of the fittest. In other words, they became "better" at getting used to their environment after some time. But what did the Bible say after God created the plants, animals, and humans? (Hint: See Genesis 1:12, 21, 25, and 31.)

   (**Answer:** *"And God saw that it was good."*)

   At the end of His creation work, the Bible says God looked over everything He made. He saw everything was very good (Genesis 1:31). They didn't need to evolve into something else.

Summary

God's original creations were *very good*—they did not become "better" through evolution and natural selection. Simpler life forms cannot become complex animals and human beings without an intelligent being like God.

1-3 Theory Buster: Evolution

Truth to Remember

We did not evolve from any other creatures on Earth.

God designed and created us according to His image.

Then God looked over all he had made, and he saw that it was very good!

Genesis 1:31

1-3 Theory Buster: Evolution

FACT CHECK

How about Ape-men, such as Lucy and Neanderthals?

Weren't they the "missing link" between the ape and men in biology and history books? To find the answers that involve digging facts, theories, and a biblical worldview, check out Dr. Steve and Ruth Carter's explanation in their book *I Really, Really, Really Want to Learn About Ape-Men*. Find the link in the Notes section.[5]

1-4

Theory Buster: We're Relatives with Chimps!

1-4 Theory Buster: We're Relatives with Chimps!

PURPOSE
To learn about DNA as instructions for life. To investigate whether humans and chimps shared the same common ancestor or were uniquely created by God.

Icebreaker

- Have you ever read in science books or heard in school that "humans have the same **common ancestors** as the great apes"? It means we have the same *great-great-great-…-grea*t grandparents with chimpanzees, gorillas, and orangutans!

- In other words, scientists claim chimps are our **closest living relatives**. What do you think of this idea?

- How are we **alike** with chimps? How are we **different** from them?

Today, we will investigate how scientists came up with this idea. Before we find the answers, let's explore what makes up living things.

The Story Of DNA — The Instruction Manual for Living Things

Imagine we are visiting a huge toy factory. We will see hundreds of factory workers busily working on different things. How do they exactly know what to do? Each factory worker has a certain job, such as assembling, packaging, or delivering. The factory workers need to understand their jobs well and do them right by following the **instruction manual** (a book that tells how to do something).

Every toy factory (and any other factory) must have an **instruction manual**. It tells the factory workers how much of each thing to use, how the machines work, how to put together different parts of the toys, how to pack the finished toys, and so on.

If the instruction manual is written in English, you can most likely read it too! They will have words made of twenty-six letters in the English alphabet.

Now imagine our body is just like the toy factory. We have lots of teeny tiny parts in our body called **cells** that are like factory workers. And just like the factory workers, each cell has a special job: to see, hear, carry oxygen, digest food, and many more (More than two hundred cell types with two hundred different jobs are in our body!).

Fun fact: Did you know a small drop of blood has about four to five million red blood cells? The red blood cells travel around our body and carry oxygen to the other cells.

So, how does each cell know what job to do? The cells in our body also have an instruction manual. But of course, it is not written in English! It's written in a different language called DNA* (deoxyribonucleic acid). Instead of having twenty-six different alphabet letters, DNA has only four different alphabet letters: A, T, C, and G.

. . .

NON-BIBLICAL VIEW

Now back to the questions:

Did humans and chimps really come from the same ancestor?

Are we really the chimps' living relatives?

Scientists have thought about these questions for a very long time. So, they did some investigation. They looked at both humans' and chimps' DNA, just like comparing different instruction manuals from two factories.

To their surprise, the instruction manuals (DNA) of humans and chimps are similar! In fact, they are almost exactly the same. The difference is only 1–2%.[1] (It means only one to two letters are different in every one hundred letters.) How come the instruction manuals of humans and chimps look so alike?

---

*__DNA__ is a special molecule that tells the cells what to do. *See Fact Checks section for more information about DNA.*

1-4 Theory Buster: We're Relatives with Chimps!

To the scientists who believe in evolution, this makes them think evolution is true:

Humans must have evolved from the same ancestor as the chimps. Only tiny changes were made when the ancestor passed down the instruction manual.

And since humans evolved from other animals, humans are not that special.

Do you think this belief is true?

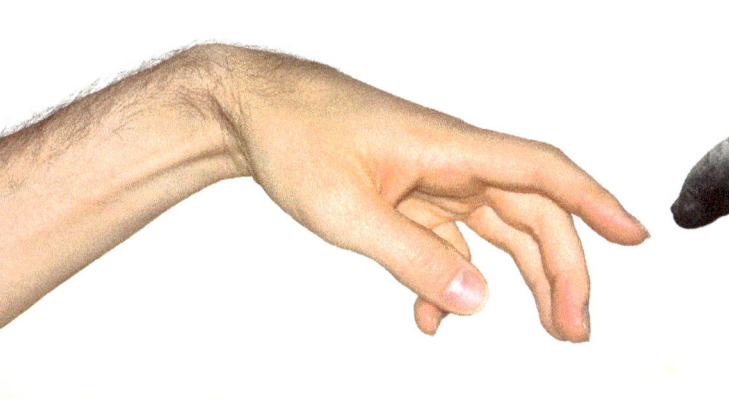

BIBLICAL VIEW

Let's look at what the Bible says. On the sixth day of creation, God created animals on land first (Genesis 1:24). Later that day, He created human beings **in His own image** to be in charge of all the wild animals on Earth—including the chimps (Genesis 1:26)! This means humans did not evolve from the chimps or their ancestors.

Genesis 2:7 also tells about how God created the first human, Adam. God "formed the man [Adam] from the dust of the ground. He breathed the breath of life into the man's nostrils, and the man became a living person." God took special care in creating the first humans, Adam and Eve! Humans are the most special among all God's creations because God made us in His own image.

Now, how can four letters of DNA make something that has so many parts and little details as a human body? How do chimps who can't talk like us and don't look like us have very similar instruction manuals to ours? Let's do an activity to answer these questions.

1-4 Theory Buster: We're Relatives with Chimps!

Activity
DNA Alphabet

MATERIALS

- One of the following materials with four different colors (at least twenty pieces of each color):
    - » beads
    - » pom poms
    - » colorful cereals (such as Fruit Loops) or candies
    - » building blocks of similar size (such as LEGO)
- String or pipe cleaners (optional—if using beads or cereals)

Colorful Beads
String

INSTRUCTIONS

1. Sort the materials into four groups of the same color.

2. Using only one color at a time, work together to build a tower using building blocks or string together beads/cereals for each color. If using pom poms/candies, lay them side by side on the table. Your family should have four creations of single-colored materials.

3. Compare the different creations. Note how many possible patterns can be made with one color only. *(There should be only one possible pattern.)*

4. Break apart the creations and sort the materials by color into four different groups again.

5. Take five pieces of each color and put it in one group. Repeat this until you have four groups of materials. Each group should have a total of twenty pieces of four different colors.

6. Build or string together the pieces using these four different colors in any patterns. If you have a family of four or fewer, each person can work on one group of materials. If you have more family members, pair up some family members to work together.

7. Compare the different creations. Note the combination and order of colors.
Ask children: *"Are there any creations with exactly the same pattern and order?" "Can you try making a different pattern next time?"*

8. If time allows, make as many different combinations as possible.

1-4 Theory Buster: We're Relatives with Chimps!

1. Using four different colors, were there any creations from our activity with exactly the same color combination? If we have unlimited time, how many different combinations can we make altogether?

   (*Answer:* *There are so many ways to make different combinations of four colors. We only used twenty building blocks. Imagine if we used different numbers of building blocks. The possibilities are endless! If we change just one building block, it will turn into a new creation.*)

   Each color we used today is like one DNA alphabet letter. Remember, we have four DNA alphabet letters. Like our creations, the four DNA letters can be arranged in many different ways.

2. Do you think the right order of the DNA alphabets is important? Why?

   (*Answer:* *The right order of DNA alphabets is crucial because it is an instruction manual for living things. A small change in DNA can mean different things.*)

   Like the instruction manual in the factory, the letters and the words must be put in the right order. Only then will they make sense and let the factory workers understand them.

3. Scientists who study DNA have discovered many new things. Technologies have gotten better, and more tools are available. Scientists actually found more differences between human and chimp DNA than years before.

   (Note to older children: In 2018, scientists found out human and chimp DNA differences are not just 1–2%, as found in 2005.[2,3] Our DNA is actually **more than 15% different** from the chimps'!)

1-4 Theory Buster: We're Relatives with Chimps!

Which one makes more sense: the old data with only little difference (1–2%) or the newer data with a bigger difference?

*(**Answer:** The newer data with a bigger difference in the instruction manuals is a more reasonable explanation for many differences between us and the chimps.)*

4. You might still wonder: "Only 15% difference? It doesn't sound like a big difference. How about the rest of the DNA? It seems like we are more similar to the chimps than we think!" How would we explain this?

*(**Answer:** Well, chimps and humans do share many similar instructions in our DNA. After all, we are both mammals. Some body functions are similar in mammals, such as giving birth to the young ones, nursing the babies, and breathing through the lungs.)*

However, such great similarities do not prove we came from the same ancestors. **Similar designs** can explain this too. An engineer uses many of the same raw materials and building plans to make different types of machines. For example, airplanes and helicopters are made from mostly the same material (metal). Still, they have very different functions and abilities.

So, it's more likely humans and chimps were **designed by the same Creator**. This Creator used the same raw materials and building blocks for life.

Summary

Humans and chimps do not share a common ancestor. Instead, we share a *common Creator* who is smarter than any person. With only four alphabet letters of life, He can code many different parts of living things with their special functions. Who would be the best Engineer of life? Our almighty God!

1-4 Theory Buster: We're Relatives with Chimps!

Truth to Remember

Humans are a unique creation, made in God's own image to have a special relationship with Him.

Then God said,
"Let us make human beings
in our image, to be like us...."

Genesis 1:26

FACT CHECK

DID YOU KNOW?

- There are more than 30 trillion cells in the human body.

- There are over 200 types of cells in the human body, and that means 200 different jobs!

- The DNA sequence is often called the "genetic code." It is similar to a computer programming code telling a computer what to do. (The genetic code is the set of rules living cells use to translate information encoded within genetic material—either DNA or RNA.)

- DNA is not just flat and boring. It looks like a beautiful, curved 3-D ladder called a "double helix." The rungs on the ladder are made of a pair of DNA alphabet letters (A, T, C, and G).

BILL GATES (A SOFTWARE DEVELOPER AND CO-FOUNDER OF MICROSOFT):

"DNA is like a computer program but far, far more advanced than any software ever created."[4]

JOHN SANFORD (A CORNELL UNIVERSITY GENETICIST)

has shown in several studies that the genetic makeup of all living creatures shows no signs of evolving or getting better. Instead, it is slowly degenerating.[5]

NOTE: For lesson 1-5, prepare the activity at least 1.5 hours before the lesson. The preparation will include about an hour baking time.

1-5

Dinosaurs and Dragons

1-5 Dinosaurs and Dragons

NOTE: Prepare for the activity at least one and a half hours before the lesson. Today's activity is optional. It will provide a fun activity to do as a family, especially those with younger kids.

PURPOSE
To investigate the existence of dinosaurs in the Bible.

Icebreaker

- Imagine humans and dinosaurs were living together, side by side. What do you think would happen?
- If these dinosaurs won't eat you alive, and you could pick any dinosaur as a pet, which one would you choose? Why?

1-5 Dinosaurs and Dragons

Did dinosaurs really exist? If yes, how come the Bible has never mentioned the word "dinosaurs" even once? Let's investigate!

Dinosaur fossils have been found all over the world.

Fossils are the remains or trace of a living animal or plant from a long time ago, such as animal bones, footprints, shells, or others. They give scientists clues about the past.

NON-BIBLICAL VIEW

If you are a huge fan of dinosaurs, then you probably know some dinosaur facts, such as:

- They *evolved* from one-celled life forms. (Do you remember what "evolved" means? How about an example of a simple, one-celled life form?)
- Dinosaurs lived millions of years ago—long before the first humans were alive.
- No human being ever lived with dinosaurs.[1,2]

Scientists also believe Earth is 4.5 billion years old.[3] Written out that would be

4,500,000,000 years ago.
(Show how many zeros there are to the younger kids.)

That's a super long time ago! Are these facts true?

NOTE TO PARENTS

There are debates among Christians about how to interpret the six-day period of creation, and hence there are two views about the age of Earth: the "**Old Earth**" (Earth is billion years old) and the "**Young Earth**" (Earth is a few thousand years old) views.

In this book, we follow the Young Earth view, which takes the number of days in the creation account literally (twenty-four hours in a day). However, some great Christian scientists who believe in the biblical creation account argue that the Earth is old, but humanity's presence on Earth is relatively recent (10,000–30,000 years). According to them, the word "day" (the Hebrew word *yôm*, Strong's #3117)in the Bible is an era or long time period.[4]

Discussion about the evidence supporting these two views is beyond the scope of this book. Regardless of the different views, both agree that God created the planet Earth, and He has a master plan for humanity.

BIBLICAL VIEW

Rather than billions of years, the Bible tells us Earth's age is only a few thousand years old. How do we know this age? Well, God gives us a timeline in the Bible as a clue!

> Along with things scientists found in different places, we know Earth is around 6,000 years old today.

(See "How old is Earth according to the Bible?" in the Fact Check section for a more detailed calculation.)

Previously, we learned God is the Creator and intelligent Designer behind the universe and everything in it. He made everything in six days! The Bible also tells us God created the land animals on day six. As **most dinosaurs were land animals, they were made on day six**—along with other land animals, Adam, and Eve (Genesis 1:24–27). Knowing these truths, dinosaurs did not exist millions of years ago. They were here thousands of years ago when God created the animals on Earth.

> Suppose humans and dinosaurs lived side by side in the garden of Eden. Won't the carnivores (the meat-eating animals) chomp off Adam and Eve's heads the minute the dinosaurs saw them?

The Bible tells us dinosaurs were at first *plant-eaters* like all other creatures on Earth (Genesis 1:30). This includes the T-Rexes. *Wait, what? Are you telling me these beasts with teeth six inches long were actually plant-eaters?* Well, yes! Many sharp-toothed animals on Earth only eat plants and fruits. Some examples are fruit bats, pandas, and vampire deer. So, plant-eating T-rexes? It's very possible!

After sin entered the world and the great flood in Noah's time happened, some animals turned into carnivores, including many dinosaurs.[5,6]

1-5 Dinosaurs and Dragons

If these biblical views are right, why can't we find the word "dinosaur" in the Bible?

The answer is the same way we can't find the words "iPad," "Tesla," or "YouTube" in the Bible. The word "dinosaur" was not invented until 1841 by Richard Owen.[7] This word means "terrible lizard."

During the biblical time, the name for dinosaurs was the Hebrew word *tannin*, which means "serpent, **dragon**, or sea monster."[8] So, the words "dinosaurs" and "dragons" actually mean the same thing in the Bible!

We will dig into the Bible to find sightings or mentions of dragons and dinosaurs later. But before that, let's have some fun and pretend to be paleontologists (people who study fossils). In fact, we have a fossil site ready today. Let's get to work!

Activity
Digging Dinosaur Fossils

MATERIALS
- Two cups of cornstarch
- One cup of water
- Medium-sized oven-safe container
- Dinosaur toy figures (can sometimes be found in dollar stores)
- Other small materials, such as rocks or gems (optional—for added fun)
- Digging tools, such as toy hammers, toothbrushes, paintbrushes, plastic knives, or other tools safe for kids.
- Old newspaper or tray (optional—to contain the mess)

INSTRUCTIONS

Preparation before the lesson (1.5 hours):

1. Mix two cups of cornstarch and one cup of water to make "oobleck" in an oven-safe container. Use approximately twice as much cornstarch as water. If the mixture becomes too soupy, add more cornstarch. If it becomes too thick, add more water.

2. Put dinosaur toy figures (and optional rocks or gems) into the oobleck. Push down the dinosaurs as much as possible until they are buried. You can separate the dinosaurs into different containers of oobleck if you have multiple children.

3. Bake the oobleck mixture in the oven at low temperature (250°F or 120°C) for about an hour or until the mixture hardens. The oobleck is ready when it looks dry and cracks all over the surface.

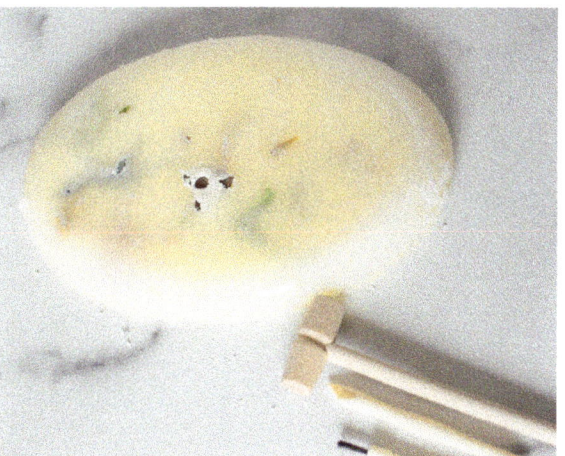

Activity with children:

Tip: *This activity can be messy. Put the dried oobleck on an old newspaper or a tray to contain the mess and for easy clean-up.*

1. Prepare digging tools for children.

2. Take out the oobleck "dinosaur fossil site" out of the container.

3. Begin digging with the tools and collect the dinosaur fossils (and other treasures).

1-5 Dinosaurs and Dragons

1. Did you know some fossil evidence proves dinosaurs lived not too long ago, instead of millions of years?[9, 10, 11, 12]

   Some paleontologists found dinosaur bones from different kinds of dinosaurs, such as a duck-billed dinosaur, a triceratops, and a T-Rex. When scientists looked more closely inside those bones, they found blood vessels that are still "springy" or flexible! And inside those blood vessels, they found what looked like red blood cells.

   Do you know what these findings mean?

   (**Answer:** *These fossils were actually pretty recent.*)

   Bones can last a long time after an animal dies, but this kind of body parts (or soft tissue) cannot last that long. Blood contains mostly water. They could not last more than hundreds of years after these animals died—maybe a thousand but **not millions of years**. Flexible blood vessels can't be in bones from millions of years ago.[13] These findings prove **the evolution and "millions of years" theories are wrong.**

2. Look at the picture here. What do you think of it?

Many scientists choose not to believe in the Bible and the story of creation. They can study the same fossils, rocks, DNA, and other things, but they may have different points of view. Wrong points of view will lead to wrong conclusions.

1-5 Dinosaurs and Dragons

3. Other than fossil evidence, a few sightings of dragons and dinosaurs are in the Bible. Let's look together! (Take turns reading the Bible verses.)

> *You split the sea by your strength and smashed the heads of the sea monsters.*
>
> *You crushed the heads of **Leviathan** and let the desert animals eat him.*
>
> *(Psalm 74:13–14)*

Some people say Leviathan is just a crocodile. Let's read Job 41 about how a Leviathan looked.

> *"Can you catch **Leviathan** with a hook or put a noose around its jaw?*
>
> *If you lay a hand on it, you will certainly remember the battle that follows. You won't try that again!*
>
> *The scales on its back are like rows of shields tightly sealed together*
>
> *Lightning leaps from its mouth; flames of fire flash out*
>
> *No sword can stop it, no spear, dart, or javelin.*
>
> *Iron is nothing but straw to that creature, and bronze is like rotten wood*
>
> *Nothing on earth is its equal, no other creature so fearless."*
>
> *(Job 41:1, 8, 15, 19, 26–27, 33)*

Does the description match a regular crocodile to you?

*(**Answer:** No, it is closer to a fire-breathing dragon!)*

4. Let's read about another creature in the Bible.

> *"Take a look at **Behemoth**,*
>
> *which I made, just as I made you.*
>
> *It eats grass like an ox.*
>
> *See its powerful loins and the muscles of its belly.*
>
> *Its tail is as strong as a cedar.*
>
> *The sinews of its thighs are knit tightly together.*
>
> *Its bones are tubes of bronze.*
>
> *Its limbs are bars of iron.*
>
> *(Job 40:15–18)*

1-5 Dinosaurs and Dragons

Some people say Behemoth is either a hippopotamus or an elephant. But have you ever seen the tails of elephants and hippos? They are tiny and don't look like a cedar tree! Can you imagine an elephant or a hippo with a tail like a cedar tree?

The creature that fits the description of a Behemoth in Job 40 is more of a **Brachiosaurus**. He has a powerful stomach, a tail like a cedar tree, and legs like iron bars.

Summary

From our findings, we can conclude a few things:

1. Earth has only been around for thousands, not billions of years.
2. Dinosaurs (also known as dragons) were created by God on day six. They did not evolve over millions of years from one-celled life forms. Dinosaurs started to live thousands of years ago when the world began.
3. Dinosaurs lived with humans for some time in the past.

1-5 Dinosaurs and Dragons

Truth to Remember

God is the Creator of all things, including the dinosaurs and the dragons in the Bible!

God made all sorts of wild animals, livestock, and small animals… And God saw that it was good.

Genesis 1:25

FACT CHECK

HOW OLD IS EARTH ACCORDING TO THE BIBLE?[14]
(The following calculation is based on the Young Earth view. See the note on page 67.)

When you read Genesis 5 and 11 about Adam's and Noah's descendants, you might wonder: *Why does the Bible have to list all the descendants, their age when they had sons, and how long they lived?*

Well, everything written in the Bible has a purpose. It gives us clues on how to calculate the age of Earth! Let's do some simple math together.

On the first day, "God created the heavens and the earth" (Genesis 1:1). That was the day the Earth was born. On the sixth day, God created Adam. So, **from the beginning of Earth to Adam**, there were **six days** total.

. . .

Genesis 5 gave a detailed list of Adam's descendants up to Noah and their ages when they had sons. For example:

"When Adam was 130 years old, he became the father of a son … He named his son Seth" *(verse 3)*.

"When Seth was 105 years old, he became the father of Enosh" *(verse 6)*.

"When Enosh was 90 years old, he became the father of Kenan" *(verse 9)*.

The list goes on until the last verse:

"After Noah was 500 years old, he became the father of Shem, Ham, and Japheth" *(verse 32)*.

If we add all the ages from **Adam to Noah** when they had their sons, the total would be **1,556 years.**

The list continues in Genesis 11:10-26, which records Noah's descendants until Abraham, along with the ages when they had their sons. Again, if we add those ages **from Noah's son, Shem, up to Abraham**, the total would be **390 years**.

So, **from Adam to Abraham**, there were 1,556 years + 390 years = 1,946 years, or **close to 2,000 years.**

. . .

Whether Christian or non-believers, most scholars would agree **Abraham** lived in about 2,000 B.C. or **2,000 years before Jesus Christ** was born.[15] (B.C. stands for "Before Christ" and means the number of years before the birth of Jesus Christ.)

Jesus's birth marked the beginning of the A.D. calendar system we use today. The traditionally accepted year of Jesus' birth is labeled A.D. 1. (A.D. stands for the Latin words *Anno Domini* or "Year of our Lord.") So, **Jesus Christ was born about 2,000 years before today.**

. . .

In summary, let's add the following:

```
  6 days (from the beginning of Earth to Adam)
~2,000 years (from Adam to Abraham)
~2,000 years (from Abraham to Jesus)
~2,000 years (from Jesus until today)          +
_____

~6,000 years TOTAL
```

So, according to the Bible, **Earth has only been around for thousands, not billions of years.**

NOTE: For lesson 1-6, prepare the activity before the lesson. Freezing three different layers of colored water may take two days.

1-6

Where Did All the Dinosaurs Go?

1-6 Where Did All the Dinosaurs Go?

NOTE: Prepare for the activity at least two days before the lesson.

PURPOSE
To investigate the extinction of dinosaurs.

Icebreaker

No more dinosaurs are roaming around our neighborhood today. What do you think happened to the dinosaurs?
Take a wild guess!

(Answer: Here's what people think:
- *Dinosaurs starved to death.*
- *They died from overeating.*
- *They were poisoned.*
- *They became blind from cataracts and could not reproduce.*
- *Mammals ate their eggs.*
- *Other reasons are volcanic dust, poisonous gases, comets, sunspots, meteorites, mass suicide, constipation, parasites, shrinking brain, slipped discs, or changes in the air composition.)*

1-6 Where Did All the Dinosaurs Go?

We've looked together how dinosaurs lived side-by-side with humans for some time before they went extinct (died out).

But, where did all these magnificent creatures go?

• • •

NON-BIBLICAL VIEW

Let's hear what scientists believe happened to the dinosaurs:

- Most scientists believe an *asteroid** fell from outer space onto Earth and wiped out the dinosaurs. (This makes us wonder: If an asteroid hit the Earth, why did only dinosaurs become extinct while other animals survived?)
- Many believe some dinosaurs *evolved* into birds!
- British scientists recently said dinosaurs "gassed" themselves to death.[1] Dinosaurs gave out too much gas (called "methane")—enough to cause severe climate change and finally wiped out all dinosaurs. (Yep, death by farts!)

BIBLICAL VIEW

What does the Bible say about what happened to the dinosaurs and dragons? In Genesis 6–8, the Bible says God sent a huge flood to destroy Earth because "the earth had become corrupt and was filled with violence" (Genesis 6:11). Noah was the only person living on Earth then who was obeying God! Only Noah, his family, and animals of each kind survived inside an ark.

Some people believe *all* dinosaurs drowned during this period. But actually, God told Noah to bring *every living thing, two by two,* into the ark (Genesis 6:19–20). That means the dinosaurs too! Now I know what you're thinking:

How could these gigantic creatures fit inside an ark?

First, remember the picture of the ark we often see in children's books? A little, cramped boat with giraffes' heads sticking out in the back. It's not drawn in the right size!

***Asteroid** is a rocky object that circles the sun.

The real ark in Genesis 6:14–16 was actually **huge**. It's as long as one and a half football fields, as wide as two school buses next to each other, and about three stories high. Now imagine how enormous it was. It could really fit a lot of big animals!

Second, God ordered Noah to take two of each animal *kind*, not species or specific breed. For example, Noah did not take four hundred pairs of different breeds of dogs (like the Poodle, German Shepherd, Chihuahua, etc.) into the ark; he just needed a pair of the dog kind.[2] For dinosaurs, out of many different varieties, there were only about **sixty to eighty kinds of dinosaurs**.[3] So that means Noah did not need that many dinosaurs to fit inside the ark.

Lastly, on average, dinosaurs in those days were about the size of a small adult African elephant (some were even as small as chickens!).[4] For some dinosaurs that could grow really big, God would have sent the younger adults to fit easily into the ark. The young adults would eat less, sleep more, and live longer to reproduce after the flood.[5]

So, did the dinosaurs make it into Noah's ark? Yes! The things we talked about just now made a lot of sense, didn't they?

However, people who believe in evolution disagree that the great flood ever happened in the first place. When they studied the layers in the Earth's crust, they did not see the proof of a great flood. They think the layers show how animals evolved in the past.

Today, we will put on our paleontologist hats again and look at the different layers in the Earth's crust. We will then learn how the fossils found in these layers point to the great flood, not evolution.

1-6 Where Did All the Dinosaurs Go?

Activity

Three-Layered Fossil Ice Block

MATERIALS

- A tall plastic container at least five inches high with a wide opening
    - **Warning:** *Do not use a glass container since water expands as it freezes and may break the glass container.*
- Three different colors of food coloring
- Animal toy figures from the following five groups:
    - » Sea animals (fish, octopus, etc.)
    - » Amphibians (frogs)
    - » Modern mammals (monkeys, dogs, etc.)
    - » Reptiles (snakes, crocodiles)
    - » Dinosaurs

  You may also draw or paint these animals on small flat stones from your yard. To do this, you will need small flat stones and markers or acrylic paints.
- Digging tools, such as toy hammers, spoons, or any other tools safe for children
- A large tray or baking dish (to contain the melted ice)
- Warm water in squirt bottles or cups (optional—to speed up the melting process)
- Salt (optional—to speed up the melting process)
- Three pieces of paper. Write the following geological eras on the paper:
    - » "Paleozoic Era = Old Life"
    - » "Mesozoic Era = Middle Life"
    - » "Cenozoic Era = New Life"

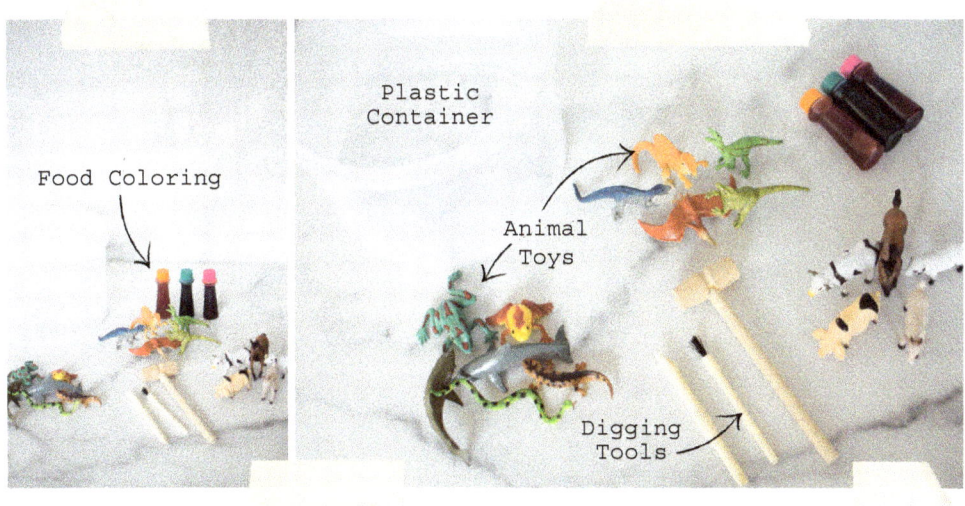

INSTRUCTIONS

Preparation before the lesson (two to three days before activity with children):

1. If you don't have animal toy figures, draw or paint animals from each of the five groups on flat stones (one animal on each stone).

2. Fill one-third of the plastic container with water and add a few drops of food coloring (any color). Mix well to get a uniform color. (The order of the color doesn't really matter, but make sure every layer has a different color to show different fossil eras.)

3. Put the **sea creature, amphibian, and reptile** toy animals/stones in the first layer. These are the fossils from the **"Paleozoic Era."**

4. Freeze the first layer.

5. After the first layer has frozen, put the **dinosaur** toy animals/stones in the second layer. These are the fossils from the **"Mesozoic Era."**

6. Put enough water into the container to make the second layer. Add a few drops of food coloring in a different color from the first one. Mix well to get a uniform color.

 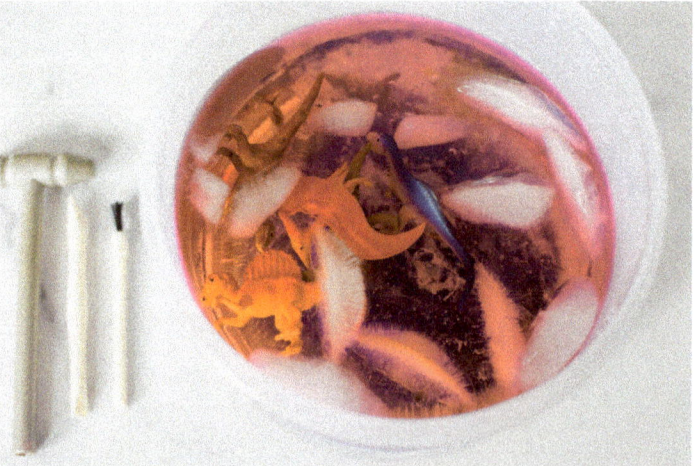

1-6 Where Did All The Dinosaurs Go?

7. Freeze the second layer.

8. Lastly, put the **modern mammal** toy animals/stones into this last layer. These are the fossils from the **"Cenozoic Era."**

9. Fill up the last third of the container with water. Put a few drops of food coloring (in the last color). Mix well to get a uniform color.

10. Freeze this last layer.

11. After the three layers have frozen, you will have a three-layered ice block containing fossils from different eras.

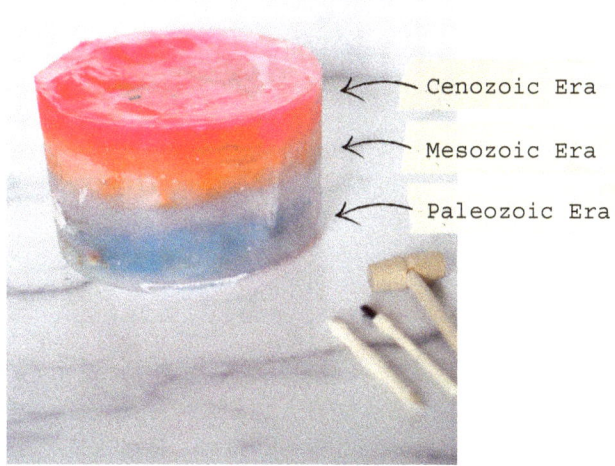

← Cenozoic Era
← Mesozoic Era
← Paleozoic Era

Activity with children:

1. Take the ice block out of the container and put it into a larger container or baking dish. You may need to run it under warm water to loosen the edge of the ice block.

2. Observe the layers together and go to *discussion points 1 and 2*.

3. Dig out the fossils with toy hammers, spoons, or other safe digging tools. Squirt warm water or sprinkle salt on the ice block to speed up the melting process.

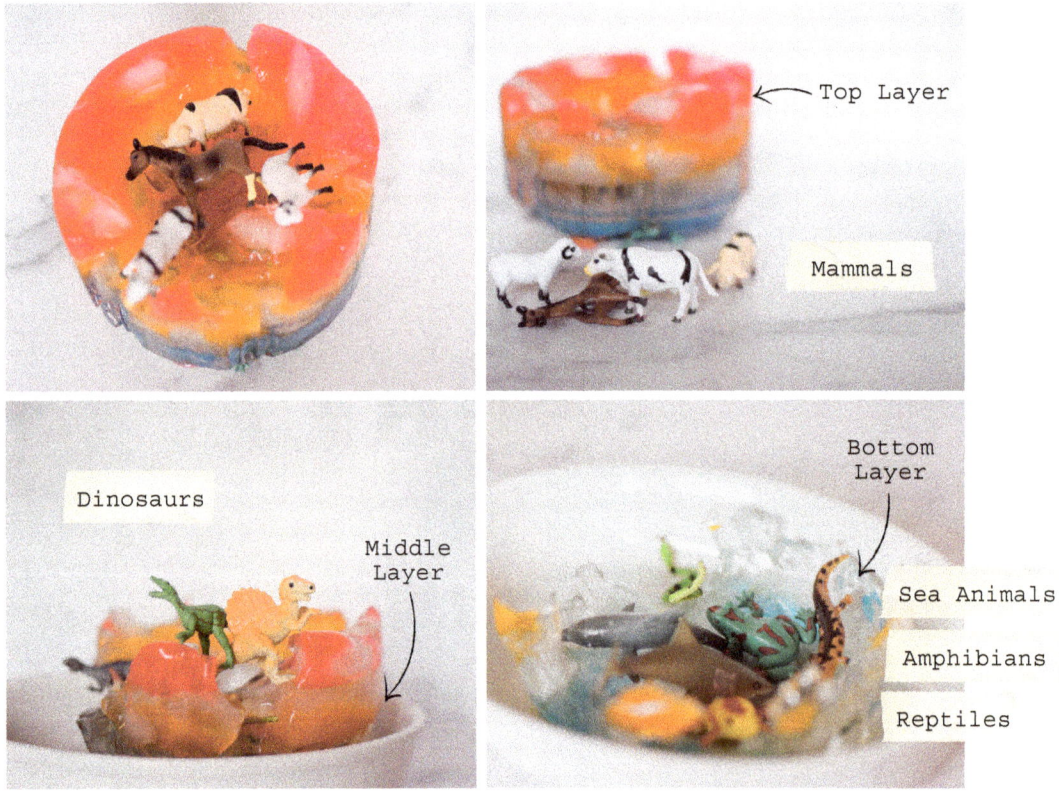

4. Collect the animal toys/stones found in each layer and group them based on geological eras.

5. Continue with the rest of the discussion points.

1-6 Where Did All the Dinosaurs Go?

Discussion

1. Let's observe these layers together. How many layers do you see in the ice block?

   Each layer of the ice block marks an era or period of history. After the great flood, there were thousands of layers formed in the Earth's crust. Scientists grouped the layers into three major groups, based on the fossils found in each rock layer: **Paleozoic Era** ("old life"), **Mesozoic Era** ("middle life"), and **Cenozoic Era** ("new life").

   (Show the labels of three geological eras to the children.)

2. Evolutionists do not believe in the great flood history. They think each layer was formed slowly over millions of years: the oldest layers at the bottom and the newest layers on top. Can you try to put these labels in order?

   (After putting the labels in order, continue with activity steps 3–5.)

3. What kinds of animals did you find in each layer?

   *(**Answer:**
   - The bottom layer, Paleozoic Era, has the fossils of sea animals, amphibians, and reptiles.
   - The middle layer, Mesozoic Era, has dinosaurs' fossils.
   - The top layer, Cenozoic Era, has modern mammals' fossils.)*

4. Why do you think scientists named the bottom layer as "old life," the middle layer as "middle life," and the top layer as "new life"?

   *(**Answer:** When evolutionists look at the fossils in these layers, they assume this is the evidence of evolution! Animals on the bottom had evolved slowly over millions of years into creatures buried above them.*

So, the oldest animals were the ones in the bottom layer [sea animals, amphibians, and reptiles]. Then, they evolved into the animals buried in the next layers above them [dinosaurs], and finally, the most recent ones [modern mammals]).

5. However, now we all know better! Which event from the Bible could explain these rock layers and fossils?

   *(**Answer:** The great flood in Noah's time.)*

   During the great flood, water covered the entire earth and killed all the animals, except the ones in Noah's ark. The strong, fast-moving water picked up and carried loose rock and soil materials across the continents. These materials settled to make rock layers, burying the dead animals in them.

   Sea animals were buried first since they lived in the ocean. Then, smaller amphibians and reptiles were buried next because they sank when they died. Dinosaurs were in the middle layer since they were bigger. They could also run to higher grounds to escape the rising water at first. And finally, mammals were in the top layer since they tend to float when they die. **These fossils do not tell the story of evolution; they simply tell us the story of the great flood.**[6]

6. Coming back to our question earlier: Where did all the dinosaurs go? What happened to them after the flood?

   *(**Answer:** The dinosaurs that survived the flood simply went extinct, just like other animals that became extinct after the great flood. Saber-toothed cats, woolly mammoths, and dodo birds are some examples.[7])*

   The dinosaurs might die out after the flood because of several reasons: lack of food, more volcanic eruptions, change in weather patterns, cooler weather during the Ice Age, or hunted by humans.[8]

   (See the Fact Check section for the records of dinosaurs living alongside humans after the flood.)

Summary

The dinosaurs did not go extinct from an asteroid hit. Based on the Bible, some dinosaurs made it into the ark, while many others did not live through the flood. The dinosaurs that died in the flood were drowned, buried, and became fossils. The dinosaurs who survived the flood made it to the other side of history. They lived alongside humans for many years. Finally, they died and went extinct.

1-6 Where Did All the Dinosaurs Go?

Truth to Remember

Many dinosaurs died during the flood, while some made it inside the ark.

After the flood of Noah, they lived alongside humans and later went extinct.

Bring a pair of every kind of animal —a male and a female— into the boat with you to keep them alive during the flood.

Genesis 6:19

1-6 Where Did All the Dinosaurs Go?

FACT CHECK

WHAT HAPPENED TO THE DINOSAURS THAT MADE IT TO THE ARK AND SURVIVED THE GREAT FLOOD?

They lived alongside humans for quite a long time. Remember that dinosaurs were called dragons? These creatures were consistently recorded by people from different cultures and continents. People from **all over the world** who never had contact with each other had stories, carvings, paintings, and pictographs describing very similar animals.[9]

America

Native Americans made a lot of pictures depicting dinosaurs: **three-horned dinosaurs** (in Montrose County, CO), **a sauropod dinosaur** (under the Kachina Bridge at Natural Bridges National Monument, Utah), and **a pterosaur** (in the San Rafael Swell, Utah).

Northern England

At Carlisle Cathedral in Northern England, there is a tomb of Bishop Richard Bell, who died in 1496. Scientists found brass carvings of **dinosaurs** on his tomb in this fifteenth-century cathedral.

France

The city of Nerluc in France was renamed in honor of a **dragon** that was slain there. It was described as being bigger than an ox with long, sharp, pointed horns on its head. (It could be a **Triceratops**.)

1-6 Where Did All the Dinosaurs Go?

Italy

A Roman mosaic from the second century A.D. showed **long-necked dinosaurs**.

Middle East

Historians Aristotle and Herodotus reported flying **dragons** and **reptiles**, just like "the flying fiery serpent" in Isaiah 30:6 (ESV). Herodotus said in Book 2, "Winged serpents are said to fly from Arabia at the beginning of spring, making for Egypt. The serpents are like water-snakes. Their wings are not feathered but similar to wings of a bat." (They could be **Pterodactyls**.)

Egypt

A famous Egyptian tablet ("the Great Hierakonpolis Palette") showed **two long-necked dragons/dinosaurs** that looked a lot like **Brachiosaurus**.

Libya

St. George was known to kill a **dragon** around 275 A.D. The description of the dragon he killed fits a **Baryonyx** dinosaur. In the same region (Libya), Baryonyx fossils were found.

China

Marco Polo, who lived in China for seventeen years around 1271 A.D., reported the emperor raised **dragons** to pull his chariots in parades.

Cambodia

In a Cambodian temple called "The Temple of Khmer" (built around 1,100 years ago), there was a carving of a **dragon** who looked like a **Stegosaurus**.

Australia

In Australia, a famous Aboriginal drawing of a creature named "Yarru" looks just like the dinosaur **Plesiosaurus**.

1-7

God Made Boys and Girls

1-7 God Made Boys and Girls

PURPOSE
To learn about God's original plan in creating human beings as male and female.

Icebreaker

- What are some things boys like to do? How about girls?
- What would you like to be when you grow up?
- Name some jobs that men usually do. *(For example, police officers, firefighters, lawyers, politicians, etc.)*
- Name some jobs that women usually do. *(For example, cooks, fashion designers, hairdressers, make-up artists, etc.)*

1-7 God Made Boys and Girls

Today, we will talk about God's final creation: humans. When a baby is born, usually the doctor calls out its gender, "It's a boy!" or "It's a girl!"

There are different types of boys and girls. They may have different hobbies, favorite things, and talents. Not all boys like to play with toy cars, and not all girls like to dress up in princess costumes. Does this mean boys can change their gender to be girls? How about the other way around: Can girls choose to be boys instead?

• • •

NON-BIBLICAL VIEW

Some people are not sure whether they are a boy or a girl. For example, a boy who loves to dance and has more sensitive feelings might feel that he is a girl trapped in a boy's body. Another example would be a girl who hates to wear dresses and loves to play with the boys. The world would lie to them and say they should just change their gender because we get to choose our gender based on how we *think or feel*. Here are the lies you would hear around you:

"The doctor and our parents *assign* us a gender when we're born—boy or girl. But what we feel inside might be different! Everyone gets to choose if they are a girl or a boy. No one else gets to choose for them."

NOTE TO PARENTS

This idea, known as "gender fluidity," says our gender is flexible, not fixed. Public schools all across America use either the "Genderbread Person" or "Gender Unicorn" pictures to teach this idea.

The Genderbread Person uses a gender spectrum to explain gender fluidity. The gender spectrum is like a scale to identify a person's gender. For children, we will call it the "gender identity line."

The gender fluidity idea suggests there is only one gender spectrum—with a boy on one end and a girl on the other end. It teaches that you can slide your gender from the boy's end to the girl's end and anywhere in between.

1-7 God Made Boys and Girls

The world teaches gender is a choice: We can "slide" or change our gender whenever we feel like it.

Do you see this picture here? *(Show the Genderbread Person to the kids.)* The world uses this kind of picture to show how you can "slide" your gender. Look at the gender identity line below. The world has only **one combined gender line** for boys and girls. Do you see "girls" on one end and "boys" on the other end?

Girls ←——————————————→ Boys

Here's what the world wants you to believe:

- Sometimes you may feel like a girl and want to do girly things, so you are on one end of this line. *(Point to "girls" on the end of the spectrum.)*
- Another day, you may feel like a boy and want to do boys' things, so you are on the other end of this line. *(Point to "boys" on the other end of the spectrum.)*
- At other times, you may feel unsure or somewhere in between, so you can be anywhere on the line here.

Is it true we can "slide" our gender? Does our feeling decide our gender? What does the Bible say about it?

NOTE TO PARENTS

Author Sue Bohlin explained that instead of one combined gender spectrum for both boys and girls, boys' gender spectrum is completely different and separated from girls'.[1] There is one specific spectrum for boys only and another spectrum for girls only. Check the resource by Sue Bohlin in the Notes on raising gender-healthy children.[2]

BIBLICAL VIEW

The Bible tells us God made us according to His image, **male and female**, and nothing in between (Genesis 1:27). The Bible teaches us God has a special plan for males and a special plan for females.

Do you remember about DNA? It's an instruction manual for living things. God made our DNA with instructions that tell our gender: either boy or girl.³ God made us as boys and girls on purpose, and He has a special plan for each one of us.

Now, look at the picture of the gender lines here. What's different from the gender line picture we saw earlier?

The gender lines for boys and girls here are separate.

Boys have one line, and girls have another line. We'll talk about these two lines one at a time.

Girly Girls ←——————————————————————→ **Tomboy Girls**

Rough and Tumble Boys ←——————————————————————→ **Artistic/Sensitive Boys**

GIRLS:

On one end of this line for girls are girly girls. They love everything pink and purple, twirl in their dresses, and wear make-up like moms.

On the other end of the line are girls who are tomboys. They love to climb trees and run fast with the boys. Most likely, they will cringe at having to wear a dress. These girls are often good at sports. Many are natural leaders. Girls who are tomboys can grow to become great leaders, teachers, and mothers when they truly embrace God's design.

1-7 God Made Boys and Girls

An example of a mighty woman leader in the Bible is **Deborah** (Judges 4). Deborah was a prophet and judge for Israel. Along with the Israelite men, she went to battle against the Canaanites and achieved a great victory. Being a warrior woman like Deborah does not mean she was a man trapped in a woman's body. She was fully a woman, called by God to lead others and do hard things.

BOYS:

On one end of the line for boys are the "rough-and-tumble" boys. They are athletic, noisy, and enjoy getting dirty.

On the other end of the line are boys who are sensitive and can feel things strongly. They understand others' feelings more easily and want to help people. They enjoy beauty and are usually good at art and music. These boys can also grow up to be great fathers, pastors, musicians, and many more.

An example of this type of boy in the Bible is **David**. He cared about others and animals. He was gifted in music and loved to worship God. David wrote at least half of the psalms in the Bible. He even "danced before the LORD with all his might" (2 Samuel 6:14)! Being a sensitive man who sang and danced did not make David feminine or girly. It does not mean he should change his gender to be a woman. We all know what God could do through this young shepherd boy. He single-handedly killed a nine-foot giant! David grew up to be a mighty king of Israel who defeated many enemies. He was created to be fully man. In fact, he was a man after God's own heart.

> Our gender is a gift from God.
> God chooses where on the gender line a person is,
> according to His design and purpose.

1-7 God Made Boys and Girls

Activity
Fork And Spoon Challenge

MATERIALS
- Forks and spoons
- One pack of instant ramen or noodle soup (or more for bigger families)
- Two bowls for each person
- A timer
- A tray or cookie sheet for each person (optional—to contain the mess)

Note: This activity can be messy. Use a tray or cookie sheet to contain the mess and for easy clean-up.

INSTRUCTIONS

1. Prepare instant ramen or noodle soup according to the package instructions.

2. Give two bowls to each person taking part in the challenge.

3. Transfer roughly equal portions of cooked noodles and broth into the first bowl of every player.

4. Ask the players to take their seats. Set the two bowls in front of them: a bowl of noodle soup and an empty bowl.

5. Give a spoon to each player.

    "The first challenge is to move the slippery noodles from one bowl to another with a spoon only. Remember: you have to lift the noodles to move them into the other bowl. You can't just put the two bowls close together and slide the noodles into the next bowl."

6. Set a timer for thirty seconds. Start the first challenge!

1-7 God Made Boys and Girls

7. The winner of the first challenge is the player who can move the most noodles.

8. Give a fork to each player.

   "The second challenge is to move the broth or liquid from one bowl to another with a fork only. You may not use the spoon."

9. Set a timer for thirty seconds. Start the second challenge!

10. The winner is the player who can move the most broth with a fork.

Discussion

1. What do you think of the challenge today?

2. What are the original purposes of forks and spoons?

   The maker of these forks and spoons has specific goals or purposes in mind. They want the forks to be used for eating spaghetti, noodles, salad, and so on. The spoons, on the other hand, are made to eat things like soup and ice cream.

3. There are times when we do a weird challenge, like moving slippery noodles with a spoon. That was so silly and fun, right? Does the spoon need to change its identity into a fork?

   (**Answer**: *Absolutely not!*)

   It's possible to scoop some noodles with a spoon, but it would be much easier to use a fork, wouldn't it? It's because the fork was made for that purpose.

4. There are also times when we don't have spoons around to eat our ice cream. If we only have a fork available, do we need to change it into a spoon before using it?

*(**Answer**: Definitely not!)*

It's completely okay to use a fork to scoop the ice cream because it's a change in function only. The fork is still a fork and keeps its original purpose.

Similarly, our interests, hobbies, and God-given talents might not match what people think of as "boyish" or "girly." But that doesn't mean the gender God made us is wrong, nor should we change it.

5. You might wonder about a 2-in-1 utensil, such as a "spork." Isn't it such a great invention? But have you ever actually used a spork before?

They may be nice to have, but they can't work as well as the original spoons or forks only. Forks are meant to be forks, and spoons are meant to be spoons.

God never makes mistakes in creating us in His image and giving us our gender. He even gave it to us in our DNA. Men and women are created with **equal worth in the image of God**. Like the spoons and forks, God made **males and females differently to work together and complete each other.**

Summary

We can't decide what our gender is by our feelings. The Bible says God created human beings in His own image; **male and female**, He created them. Nothing in between. God never makes mistakes. Our gender is a gift from God, and He plans to use it for amazing purposes for His kingdom!

1-7 God Made Boys and Girls

Truth to Remember

We are made according to His image: male and female, for specific purposes.

So God created human beings in his own image.
In the image of God he created them;
male and female he created them.

Genesis 1:27

1-7 God Made Boys and Girls

1-8

Living on Purpose

PURPOSE
To understand the ultimate purpose of God's creation of humans.

Icebreaker

- Grab a family picture or a mirror. Who do you look like: your brother, sister, or parents? (It could be any physical traits, such as eye color, hair, or others.)
- Are there any other things similar between you and your family members, such as how you walk, talk, or act? Do you share similar hobbies or habits?

1-8 Living on Purpose

In our last lesson, we learned that God created us in His image. Many people—young and old—have asked the questions:

Why did God make me?
What is my purpose* here on Earth?

Have you ever wondered about that too? You're not alone! People try to find their life purpose by getting rich and famous or winning awards. But they still feel empty and frustrated in the end. They don't know God has a greater purpose for their lives.

• • •

NON-BIBLICAL VIEW

Some unbelievers think God is not that great after all: *If He's great, then He won't need extra compliments or praises from us*. They argue God demands people to worship Him to add to His value—to make Him greater.

Let's hear some other thoughts about why God created humans:

- Doesn't God have enough angels to worship Him all the time in heaven? Why humans too?
- Is God so insecure that He demands praise and worship from us?
- Perhaps God is lonely and needs somebody to talk to.

Have you ever heard or thought likewise?

BIBLICAL VIEW

Let's check whether the Bible has the answer to our big questions today. In **Isaiah 43:7**, God said:

> *Bring all who claim me as their God,*
>
> *for I have made them* **for my glory.**
>
> *It was I who created them.'"*

God created humans **to bring glory to Him**. That's our purpose on Earth!

***Purpose** is the reason why something exists.

We were made in God's image to make people remember and think about God.

No other creations (including the angels) were created in His image.

What does it mean to bring glory to God?

The word "glory" means "great honor, praise, or fame." When we bring glory to God, **we show that we believe He is amazing and worthy of honor.** We do this by praising, worshiping, and expressing our love for Him. Bringing glory to God also means **telling others about Him**.

God did not create us because He was lonely or wanted someone to talk to. God is perfect and complete—and has been that way since the beginning. He doesn't need our praise and worship to make Him greater.

God wants us to tell others about Him because He loves all people. He wants humans to have a relationship with Him and to enjoy His love and kindness forever.

Let's learn from the sun and the moon to help us understand our purpose on Earth.

Activity

The Sun And The Moon

MATERIALS

- A small mirror
- A flashlight
- A stack of books (optional—to make the mirror stand upright)

Note: If this activity is done during the day, you will need to darken the room.

INSTRUCTIONS

1. Do the following experiment on a table about six feet in front of a wall.

2. Set the mirror to stand upright on the table. Use a stack of books to support it if needed.

3. Look at the following questions. Turn off the light in the room and ask the questions to children. Turn on the light again after the children have answered.

    "Can you see the mirror?"
    "How much light does the mirror give out by itself?"

4. After the light is on, say:

    "The moon is like this mirror. It cannot give off light on its own."
    "So, how can a moon look glowing at night?"

    *(**Answer:** It reflects light from the sun.)*

5. Show the flashlight to children.

    "This flashlight is like the sun as a source of light. The moon and the mirror cannot create light. They can only reflect light from the sun or the flashlight."

6. Hold the flashlight at an angle to the mirror. Turn the flashlight on. Turn off the light in the room again and observe what happens to the other side of the room. *(The mirror looks bright, and a circle of light is on the opposite wall.)*

7. Bring the flashlight closer to the mirror and see if there is any change to the reflection. *(The light reflection on the wall gets bigger and brighter as the flashlight is closer to the mirror.)*

1. What did you learn from our activity about the moon and the sun?

   *(**Answer:** Just like the mirror and the flashlight, the moon only reflects light from the sun. Without the sun, there would be no moonlight.)*

2. Let's see how today's activity relates to our purpose on Earth. Who is like the sun? And who is like the moon?

   *(**Answer:** God is like the sun or the flashlight. We are like the moon or the mirror.)*

   Just as the moon has no light on its own, we can't create our light without God. When we try to brag or get someone to say how good we are for the things we do, it's like the moon saying, "Hey, look at how cool and bright I am!" It sounds silly, right? We all know the moon's brightness actually comes from the sun.

   Our ultimate purpose on Earth is to bring glory to God—to show and tell about Him to those around us. We are meant to reflect God's light, so others can see how good God is.

3. Do you remember what happened when we brought the flashlight closer to the mirror?

   *(**Answer:** The light reflection on the wall got bigger and brighter.)*

   Likewise, as we spend more time with God and get closer to Him as our source of light, we can shine brighter. **We need to know God before we can tell others how good He is.**

4. What does it mean by "knowing God"? Think about some famous people (an athlete, an artist, or a celebrity). Do you know them?

   *(**Answer:** Yes, maybe from stories or the news.)*

   But, do we actually *know* them? Most likely not. We can't talk to them daily like we do with our family or friends. We don't know what they think, feel, or like.

   The same thing is true with God. We can know *about* God from Bible stories or what other people tell us. But we can also *know* Him when we **build a relationship with Him**. How? By inviting Him to live in us, talking to Him in prayer, and listening to Him speaking to us through His Word, the Bible. Sometimes when we pray or read the Bible, we think of something we should do differently, a nice thing to do for someone else, or someone we should apologize to. That might be God speaking to us!

   As we spend time with God, we know Him better and can tell others about Him from our experience. *(See the story of Moses and his radiant face in the Fact Check section.)*

5. The Bible says, "*whatever* you do, do it all for the glory of God" (1 Corinthians 10:31). This means honoring God at *all times*, not just every now and then. Let others see God in all our actions and words. Be it dancing, singing songs, playing sports, gymnastics…even watching television, playing games, or painting our nails, do it for the glory of God! Whether we are doing chores we don't like or helping our grumpy neighbors…do them all for the glory of God!

1-8 Living on Purpose

How can we reflect God's glory in ordinary tasks and daily life?
(**Hint:** Read **Philippians 2:14–15** NIrV.)

Do everything without complaining or arguing.

Then you will be pure and without blame.

You will be children of God without fault among sinful and evil people.

Then you will shine among them like stars in the sky.

*(****Answer:*** *The Bible says we need to* ***do everything without complaining and arguing and to live clean or blameless.*** *In that way, no one can criticize us, and we can reflect God's glory.)*

Let God shine in us, so others may want to know more about Him.

(See the Fact Check section for more ways to reflect God's glory.)

Summary

A relationship with God matters above all else in life. Without that relationship and the desire to glorify Him, our lives have no real purpose. God has unique plans and purposes for each person. But whatever those plans look like, they will ultimately result in His glory. Remember, every choice we make is a chance to glorify God! Tell and show others about God, so they can enjoy God's love and have a relationship with Him too.

Truth to Remember

Our ultimate purpose on Earth is to give glory to God—to tell and show others about Him.

So whether you eat or drink,
or whatever you do,
do it all for the glory of God.

1 Corinthians 10:31

FACT CHECK

HAVE YOU HEARD ABOUT THE STORY OF MOSES AND HIS RADIANT FACE (EXODUS 34:28-29)?

Moses wasn't aware his face had become radiant because he had spoken to God for forty days and forty nights. He spent so much time with God that his face "glowed" with God's glory. It was so bright that the Israelites were afraid at first. Moses had to put a veil over his face while talking to them!

SOME WAYS TO REFLECT GOD'S GLORY:

- Spend time with God—our light source and the One whose image we bear (John 15:5-8). We give Him glory by praying, praising, and worshipping Him.
- Accept and embrace the fact that God created us as a male or a female with a purpose to glorify Him.
- Take care of our body as a temple of God ("glorify God in your body" — 1 Corinthians 6:19-20 ESV).
  - » What kind of foods and drinks do we consume?
  - » Do we exercise enough and keep good hygiene to keep it healthy?
- Show how awesome and amazing God is through our attitudes, words, actions, and how we think. Give Him the honor, praise, and worship.
  - » Do we bring God honor in how we act and speak?
  - » Do we acknowledge God and show a thankful attitude for what He has done for us?
  - » Can others see God in the way we live our lives?
  - » Do we point others to Jesus (like the mirror and the moon)? Or do we point others to ourselves and what we have done?

1-9

God's Unique Masterpiece

1-9 God's Unique Masterpiece

PURPOSE
To show God created each of us uniquely and thought of us even before we were born.

Icebreaker

- Tell us your proudest work or creation (for example, painting, craft, LEGO structures, or others).
- How would you feel if someone ruins it?

We've learned together that God created humans in His image for a special purpose. When you meet a newborn baby, what do you think of? *Aww, what a cute baby! Look at the teeny tiny fingers!*

Today, we'll take a quick journey to see how we all began: as a baby in the mother's womb (inside the mom's belly).

A human baby grows for about thirty-eight weeks or nine months in the mom's belly. We can't see it with our eyes, but the details of how a baby grows are *mind-blowing!*

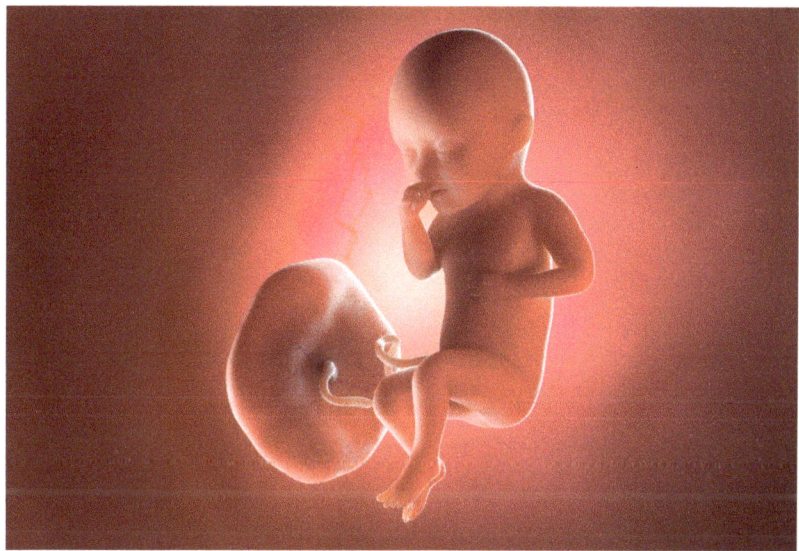

How do we know it? Scientists have done many studies on babies growing inside the mother's womb.[1] Here are some amazing facts:

- At week three, the baby's heart beats.
- At week six, the baby's brain activity begins.
- By eight weeks, fingers and toes exist.
- At week nine, a baby starts to yawn, suck his/her thumb, and stretch. The baby can bend the hip and knee if we touch the sole of his/her foot!

Can you imagine how tiny a baby is when all these things are happening? (Here's a clue: The baby is smaller than your fist!)

• • •

1-9 God's Unique Masterpiece

NON-BIBLICAL VIEW

Sadly, many people think they can just do anything and even harm the babies who are still in the mom's belly. They say unborn babies can't feel pain yet, especially when the babies are still that small; unborn babies are not real "persons" until much later (when babies can "feel" pain or after birth).[2,3]

Is it right to take away unborn babies' right to live?

BIBLICAL VIEW

The Bible says we are **God's masterpiece** (Ephesians 2:10). This means we are God's *greatest* piece of work!

A very famous masterpiece in the world is the *Mona Lisa* painting by Leonardo da Vinci. He worked on this painting of a lady for *four whole years!* That's a long time to work on a single artwork, right? Can you guess how much it's worth? In 2019, it was valued at up to $850 million.

Another well-known masterpiece is the Statue of *David* by Michelangelo. It's worth $200 million!

As we are God's masterpiece, we are worth so much more in God's eyes!

God created each of us **unique** and **special**. He began His work on us in our mom's belly. In Psalm 139:13, David said, "You made all the delicate, inner parts of my body and knit me together in my mother's womb." He also said, "Such knowledge is too wonderful for me, *too great for me to understand!*" (v. 6). Humans can never fully understand God's work.

Do you know scientists are still studying the wonders of the human body even today? There are still so many unsolved mysteries! One of them is the fingerprint. Each person has a unique fingerprint. Even identical twins don't have the same fingerprints. Now, let's observe our family's fingerprints together!

1-9 God's Unique Masterpiece

Activity
Fingerprinting

MATERIALS
- Pencil
- Light-colored paper
- Clear tape
- Magnifying glass (optional)

INSTRUCTIONS

1. Rub pencil lead over a small area on a blank sheet of paper. Do this repeatedly until there is a nice black spot of graphite from the pencil.

2. Rub your index finger across the graphite spot on the paper to transfer the graphite onto your finger.

3. Have another family member tear off about one inch (2.5 cm) of tape and stick it on the darkened tip of your finger.

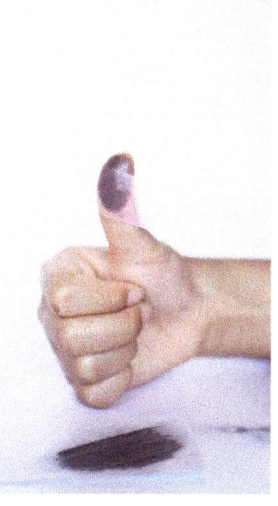

1-9 God's Unique Masterpiece

4. Remove the tape and stick it on a new sheet of paper.
5. Write the name of the fingerprint's owner and which finger it is (for example, "Lucy's left index finger").

6. Repeat steps 2 to 5 with other family members' index fingers. If time permits, you can try fingerprinting other fingers.
7. Observe the fingerprint patterns (using a magnifying glass if available).
8. Compare the fingerprints of your family and identify some basic patterns. (See examples in the picture.)

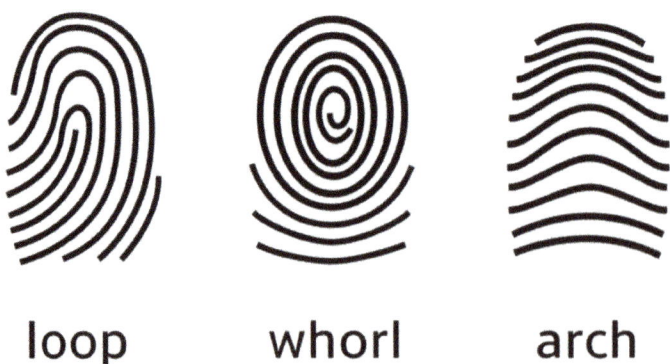

loop   whorl   arch

Discussion

1. How do the fingerprints in our family compare to each other?

   You might notice similar patterns on different fingerprints, but they will never be exactly the same. Each person's fingerprint is unique. This is like a personal signature, which will never change for the rest of our lives.

2. How do people use unique fingerprints to help them?

   (**Answer:** *Some examples are identification in criminal investigations, personal identification in electronic gadgets, such as TouchID for Apple users, and many others.*)

3. When do you think your fingerprints were formed?

   (**Answer:** *Our fingerprints were formed when we were still in our mom's belly! Fingerprints begin to* **form around the tenth week** *and are* **complete by the end of the fourth month** *of pregnancy).*[4]

   No one knows how fingerprints are formed. In fact, scientists have studied fingerprints for about 200 years! Still, they can't explain how exactly fingerprints are formed.

1-9 God's Unique Masterpiece

4. Can you imagine how big you were when your fingerprints were formed? Take a wild guess!

During week ten of pregnancy (when fingerprints start to form), a baby is **about one inch** or *as big as a strawberry.*[5] *(Show the kids how big this is and ask them to imagine how small the baby's fingers would be.)* Even when we were still as little as a strawberry, God was working on our unique fingerprints! Isn't it amazing?

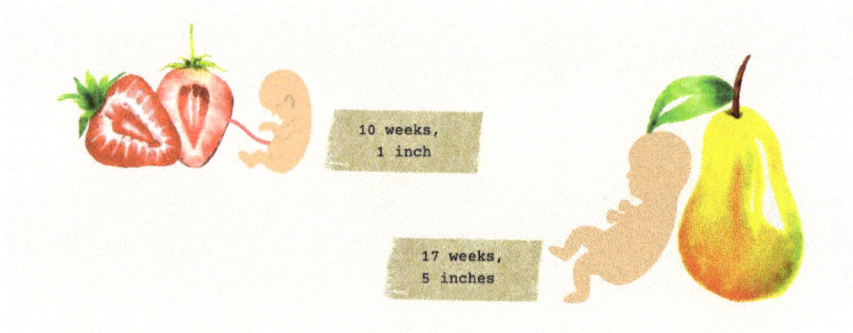

By the time our fingerprints were done (at about four-months-old in our mom's womb), we were only **about five inches long**. That's only as big as a pear!

Can you imagine how amazing God's masterpiece is? He really pays close attention to our smallest details.

5. David said to God in Psalm 139:13:

    You made all the delicate, inner parts of my body and knit me together in my mother's womb.

    Why do you think David used the word "knit" to describe God's work?

(**Answer:** *To show God took great care with forming us in our mom's belly.*)

Have you ever knitted or seen anyone knitting before? Do you think you could knit something with your eyes closed and be done in five minutes? Of course not! Knitting takes hours and days because **the details are important.** You can't just do it anyhow you like. You have to make the right measurement and calculation. God also took time to shape us, **His detailed masterpiece!**

6. If an artist has just started painting his first few strokes on a canvas, is it okay to mess around with his work? How would you feel if you just started knitting a hat and someone pulls the yarn to unravel everything you had done?

   Likewise, we should also cherish God's wonderful creation of humans—born or unborn, no matter how big or small. His work might seem unfinished when the babies are not born yet. But He has started the creation of His masterpiece no one can ever duplicate.

   (See the Fact Check section for when life begins and what the Bible says about it.)

Summary

We are not just an "accident of nature." God's wonderful work to create life begins in our mom's belly. Each of us is fearfully and wonderfully made—a special masterpiece of an amazing Creator.

Truth to Remember

I am unique.
I am God's special masterpiece.

I praise You because I am fearfully and wonderfully made

Psalm 139:14 NIV

1-9 God's Unique Masterpiece

FACT CHECK

WHEN DOES LIFE BEGIN?

At conception (also known as "fertilization"), a male sperm (from the dad) unites with a female egg (from the mom). This fusion results in a single human cell, known as a "zygote."

Many people claim human beings are not "persons" until they can feel pain or after birth. But science agrees that human life already begins at conception. A unique being comes into existence at conception. This new life has human DNA and is the offspring of human parents, so it can be described as **human life.**[6,7]

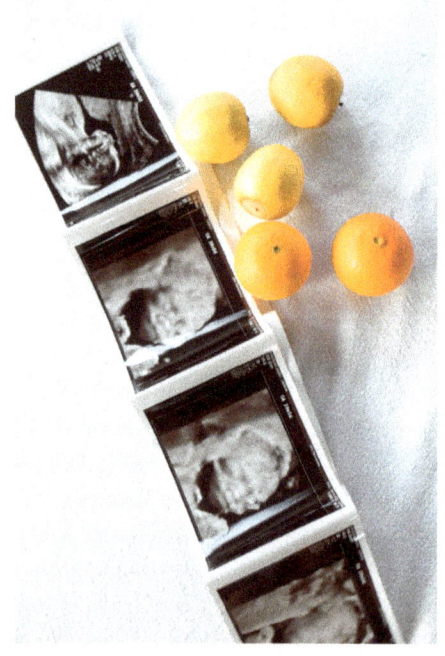

WHAT DOES THE BIBLE SAY ABOUT THE BEGINNING OF LIFE?

In Luke 1:39-45, Mary has just received the news from an angel that she would be pregnant with the Messiah (Jesus Christ). A few days later, she visited her cousin Elizabeth, who was pregnant with John the Baptist. (It was Elizabeth's sixth month of pregnancy.)

John the Baptist—an unborn baby—"jumped for joy" in his mom's womb (v. 41). He recognized the Messiah, who was also not born yet. In fact, Mary was still very early in her pregnancy. Jesus' presence also filled Elizabeth with the Holy Spirit. Just a short time after conception, an unborn baby was honored rightly by Elizabeth and her unborn child.

"According to the Bible, life is more than just potential, and it is valuable from the moment of conception. Additionally, there is no valid argument for abortion in the Biblical text."[8]

EXTRA RESOURCES:

For more Bible references and how to defend your beliefs about the life of unborn babies, check out the resources in the Notes section.[9,10]

For young children:

The Wonderful Way Babies Are Made book by Larry Christenson is a helpful resource to explain about babies, the sexual act, and reproduction in the context of families and God's plan.[11] The text is written on two different levels. On one page, the text is written for young children (up to about age eight). The facing page has more detailed information for children about nine and older.

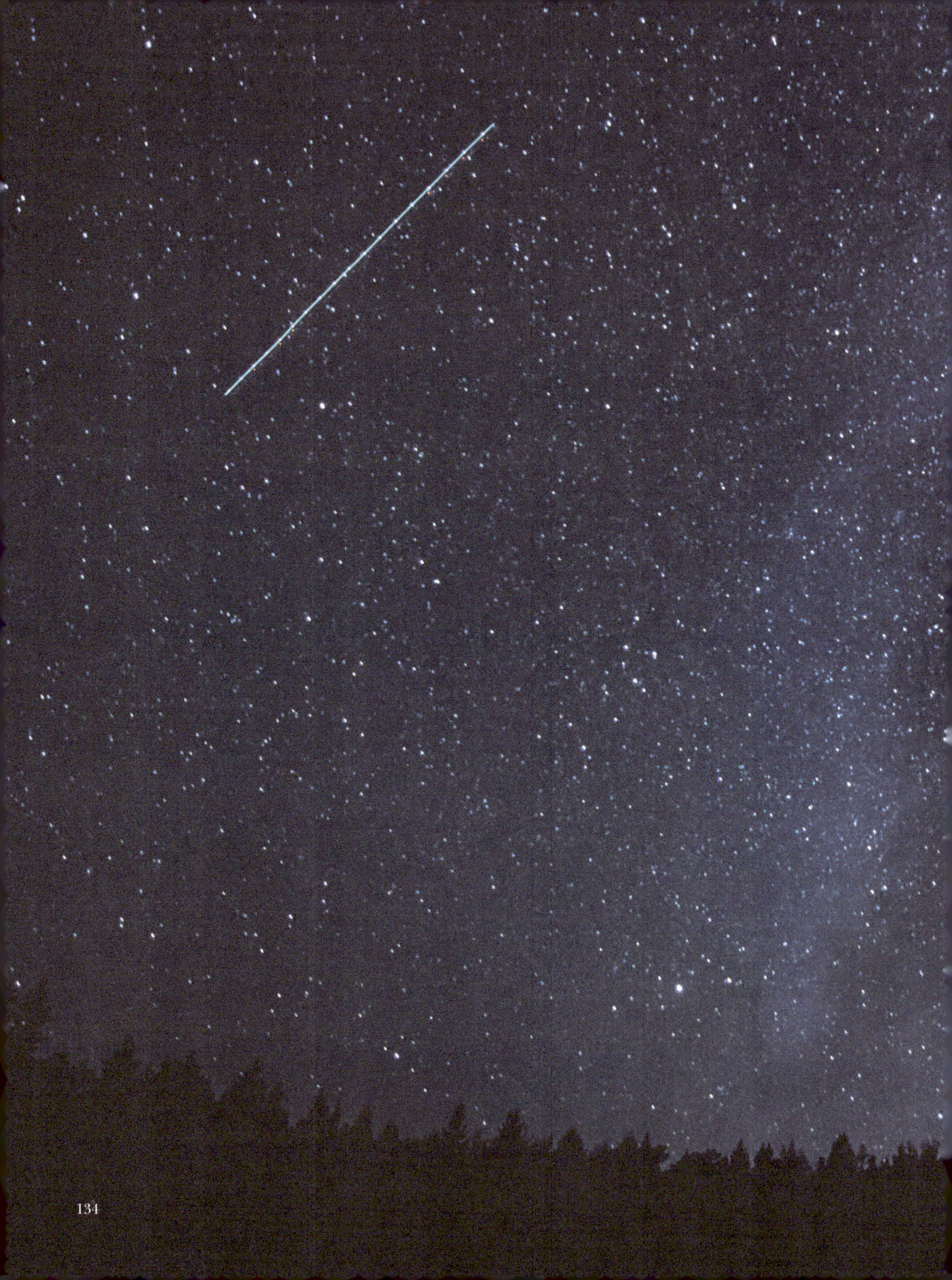

1-10

You Are Chosen!

PURPOSE
To show God cares for each one of us, and we are significant in His eyes. To understand "self-esteem" versus "God-esteem."

- Have you looked at the stars on a clear night?
- Do you know what a "constellation" is?

  A constellation is a group of stars in the sky that scientists thought looks like and is named after an animal, a person, or an object.

- Can you name some constellations?
  » *The Big Dipper, which is a part of the Ursa Major or "the Great Bear" constellation*
  » *The Little Dipper, which is a part of the Ursa Minor or "the Little Bear" constellation*
  » *Orion "the Hunter" with Orion's belt*
  » *Corona Borealis or "the Northern Crown" in Latin*

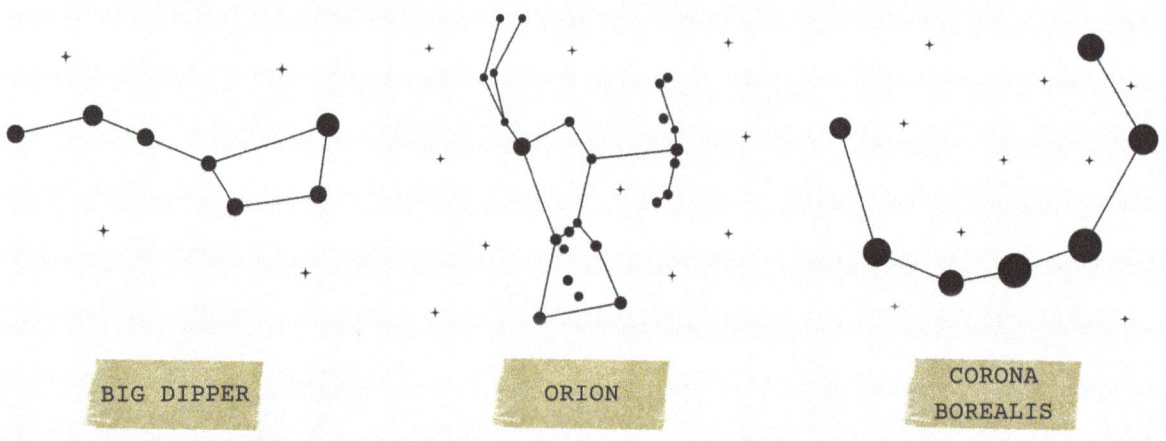

BIG DIPPER — ORION — CORONA BOREALIS

When we look into the night sky and try to count the stars, we can count tens, hundreds, or maybe thousands of stars (depending on our location and how patient we are). People who study space estimate there are 100 billion stars in the Milky Way galaxy alone.[1] Written out that would be a "1" with eleven zeros after it. That's a lot of stars!

The Bible actually compared the number of stars with the number of people living on Earth. In Genesis 15:5, God made a promise to Abraham about his descendants (the children who will be born into his family). The Lord took Abraham outside and said, "Look up into the sky and count the stars if you can. That's how many descendants you will have!"

That promise came true. Do you know how many people live in the world today? As of 2021, there are more than 7.9 billion people.[2] (Written out that would be 7,900,000,000.) And the number is still growing.

• • •

NON-BIBLICAL VIEW

Looking at this huge number and the world around us, we might feel small and not important.

Who am I among this "sea" of people? Does my life even matter?

Many people wonder about their worth or value and no longer feel confident. They struggle with low self-esteem*. Sometimes, just like one star out of billions of other stars, we might feel lost and invisible.

Do the things we have and can do decide our worth or value?

BIBLICAL VIEW

What does the Bible really say about each of us? Before answering that question, let's hear what God said to Job in **Job 38:31–33** (NIV):

> "Can you bind the chains of the **Pleiades**?
> Can you loosen **Orion's belt**?
> Can you bring forth the constellations in their season
> or lead out the **Bear with its cubs**?
> Do you know the laws of the heavens?
> Can you set up God's dominion over the earth?

Did you notice these verses mention some constellations? What are they?

> The Pleiades (also known as the "Seven Sisters" star cluster),
> Orion's belt, and the Bear with its cubs (Ursa Major and Ursa Minor).

***Self-esteem** is how someone thinks of their value.

1-10 You Are Chosen!

God created many, many stars—more than we could ever imagine! But, here's a super important truth: He placed *each one* in the right spot to form "constellations." The stars are not just out there in random places. God put them in the exact spot He wanted them, and He did it because He had a purpose for them.

In **Matthew 10:29–31**, Jesus once said to His twelve disciples:

What is the price of two sparrows—one copper coin? But not a single sparrow can fall to the ground without your Father knowing it. And the very hairs on your head are all numbered. So don't be afraid; you are more valuable to God than a whole flock of sparrows.

Our God of this universe cares so much about a small bird and places the stars in their exact positions. Can you imagine how much more valuable we are in His eyes? He cares for us ... a lot! He pays great attention to us, down to the smallest details of our lives. Even the hair on our head is numbered. God, our Creator, values us dearly and cherishes us as His own.

Our Creator defines our worth and value. We call this "God-esteem."

Let's make a constellation jar today to remind us that just like the stars, God put us carefully and purposefully in this big world.

Activity

Constellation Jars

MATERIALS

- A glass jar (wide enough to fit a small light inside)—*for each constellation jar*
- A piece of light-colored construction paper—*for each constellation jar*
- Aluminum foil
- Ruler
- String or yarn
- Scissors
- Tape
- Pushpins or bamboo skewers (or any sharp objects to poke holes)
- A piece of cardboard (optional—to protect your working surface when poking the aluminum foil)
- Pen or marker
- Battery-operated light, such as tea light, LED click light, or string light—*for each constellation jar*

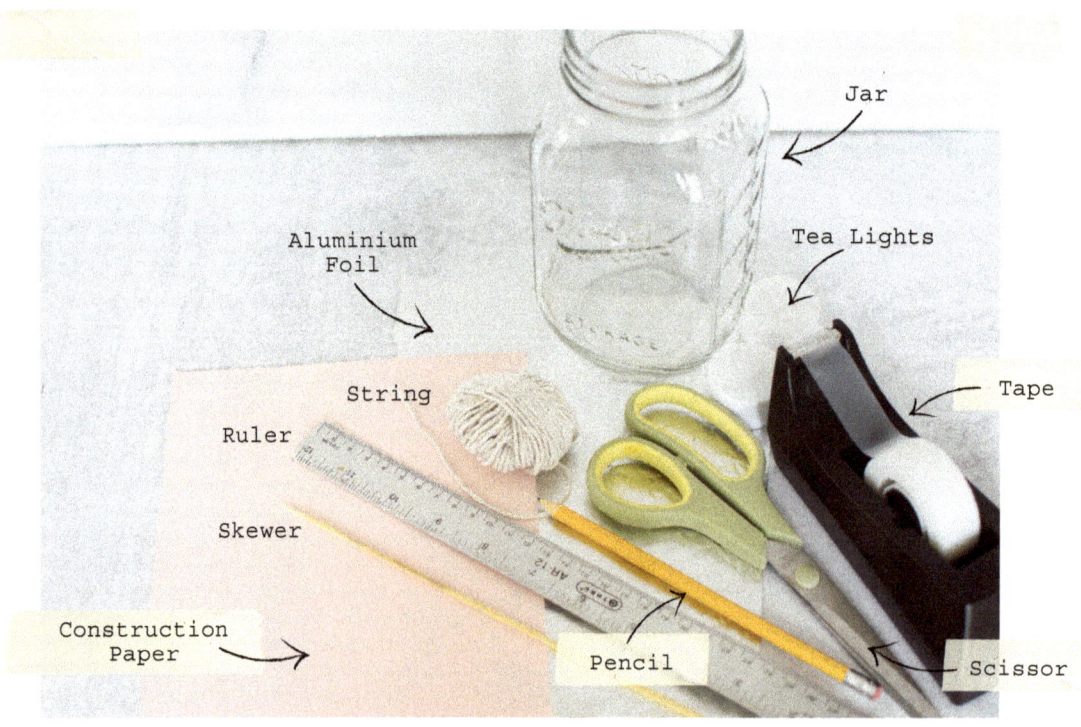

INSTRUCTIONS

1. Use a ruler to measure the height of the jar. Then, use a string to find the circumference of the jar. Wrap the string around the jar's mouth and measure its length with a ruler. Add half an inch to this circumference measurement.

2. Cut a rectangle out of construction paper based on the jar's measurements. For example, if the jar's height is five inches and the circumference is seven inches, then cut a rectangle of five by seven *and a half* inches.

3. Cover one rectangle's surface with aluminum foil (shiny side out). Leave about one-half inch extra of aluminum foil on each side. Fold the extra foil over and secure with tape.

4. Draw constellations of your choice on the foil side with a marker.

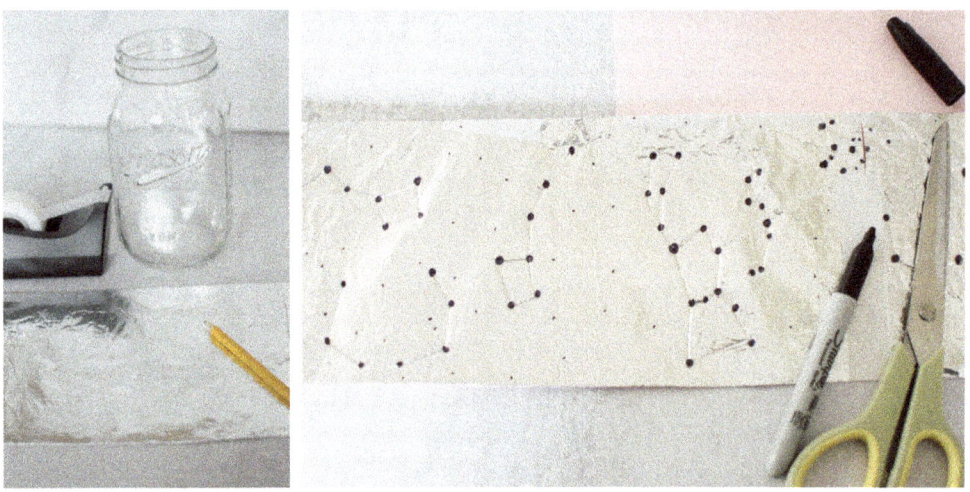

5. To create constellations, use a sharp object to poke holes through the foil sheet carefully.

   Tip: *Use a piece of cardboard underneath the foil and paper to protect your working surface. Or, try putting the foil on top of the jar to make poking holes easier.*

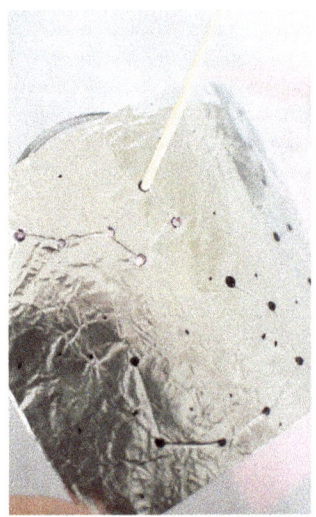

6. Use a marker to connect the constellation dots on the foil side so it's easier to see the outlines.

7. Optional: Poke smaller holes randomly to fill in the space. Make these "filler" holes smaller than the constellations', so the constellations will stand out more.

   Tip: *If the constellation holes are not big enough, enlarge the holes by poking them again from the foil side.*

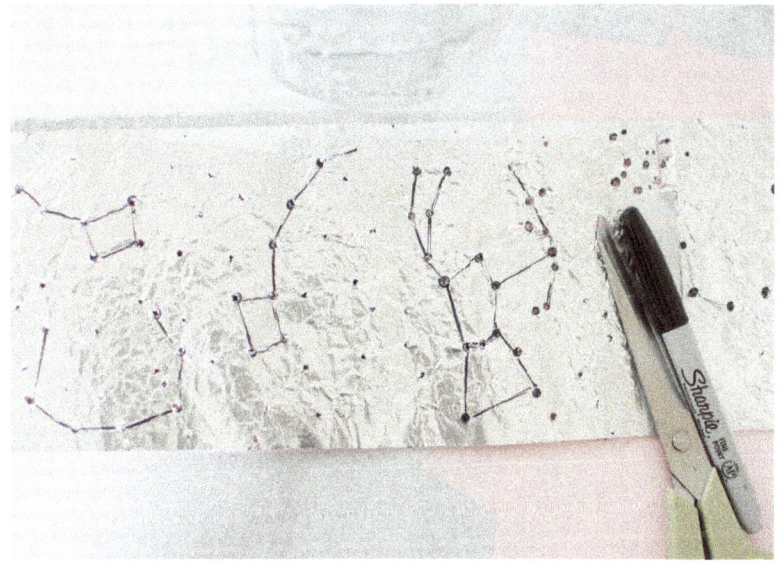

8. Roll the foil sheet to fit snugly inside the glass jar.

9. Tape the two ends of the foil sheet together and put it in the jar.

10. Turn on the battery-operated light, and place it inside the jar.

11. Screw on the jar lid.
12. Take the jar to a dark room and marvel at your newly-created constellation jar!

Discussion

1. Imagine you lived a long time ago when there was no modern compass, Google Maps, or GPS to tell directions. How would you know which direction to go? How would you travel and know your way around?

2. Do you remember the wise men's story in the Bible (Matthew 2:1–10)? These men traveled from eastern lands and wondered about the precise location of the newborn King. After talking to King Herod in Jerusalem, they discovered they were supposed to go to Bethlehem to find Jesus. But how did they know which direction Bethlehem was? (**Hint:** Read Matthew 2:9–10.)

   After this interview the wise men went their way. And the star they had seen in the east guided them to Bethlehem. It went ahead of them and stopped over the place where the child was. When they saw the star, they were filled with joy!

   (**Answer:** *There was no GPS at that time! The star showed them the way.*)

   Isn't it amazing how they could follow a star to find Jesus? The star was placed there for a great purpose: to lead people to Jesus. It is the same way with us because God put us on this Earth—at the right time and place—to point people to Him.

1-10 You Are Chosen!

3. Do you know what constellations are used for?

   (*Answer:*
   - *To help people recognize certain stars in the sky. By looking for patterns, the stars and their locations can be much easier to spot. For example, by finding Ursa Minor, it's fairly easy to spot the North Star [Polaris].*
   - *To navigate or find which direction to go [just like the wise men in the Bible]. For example, the North Star [Polaris] points in the North direction.*
   - *In ancient times, people used constellations to keep track of the calendar, so they knew when to plant and harvest crops.[3])*

   Constellations are also placed by God for special purposes. Just like these constellations, our lives are a part of a bigger picture. We are not supposed to live a selfish life, separated from others. Each of our lives connects together for God's bigger purpose.

4. If one or two stars are "missing" from a constellation, what would happen to the constellation? Will people still recognize it?

   (*Answer:* *The pattern will look different. It will be much harder to recognize a constellation if the pattern is changed.*)

   Each star in a constellation is important and significant. That one star among billions of others in the sky matters! Likewise, you are one person out of billions in the world. But you are significant and valuable in God's eyes!

5. Read Jeremiah 1:5 (MSG) about what God said to the prophet Jeremiah.

    "Before I shaped you in the womb,

    I knew all about you.

    Before you saw the light of day,

    I had holy plans for you:

    A prophet to the nations—

    that's what I had in mind for you."

Isn't it amazing to know our great God thought of us and had holy plans for us even *before* we were born?

Summary

Looking at the world around us, we might feel small and unimportant. Remember, what we have or can do does not define our worth. Our Creator defines our value, and He thinks we are priceless. He chose us to be His children. Just like the stars in the constellations, God placed each of us **in the right place, at the right time,** for a bigger purpose. He cares for us, and we are significant in His eyes.

Whenever you look at this constellation jar, remember God chose you to be His special child.

1-10 You Are Chosen!

Truth to Remember

I am special in God's eyes.
He even knows the number of hairs on my head.

*He counts the stars
and calls them all by name.*

Psalm 147:4 NIV

1-10 You Are Chosen!

Here's a list of all Truths to Remember and the memory verses from this book for a quick reference and reminders. The powerful Truths in these pages will help your family stand up against the enemy's lies. The Bible says to "repeat them again and again." Talk about them when you are at home, on the road, going to bed, and getting up (Deuteronomy 6:7). You may create a memory card for each Truth and Bible verse, ask children to write the Truths in their journals, or have a quick quiz during car rides.

1 God is the cause of the beginning of the universe.

> He made heaven and earth, the sea, and everything in them.
> He keeps every promise forever.
>
> — *Psalm 146:6*

2 Life on Earth is possible because God finely tuned it to make it just right.

> God created everything through him,
> and nothing was created except through him
>
> — *John 1:3*

3 We did not evolve from any other creatures on Earth. God designed and created us according to His image.

> Then God looked over all he had made, and he saw that it was very good!
>
> — *Genesis 1:31*

4. Humans are a unique creation, made in God's own image to have a special relationship with Him.

> Then God said, "Let us make human beings in our image, to be like us…."
>
> — Genesis 1:26

5. God is the Creator of all things, including the dinosaurs and the dragons in the Bible!

> God made all sorts of wild animals, livestock, and small animals… And God saw that it was good.
>
> — Genesis 1:25

6. Many dinosaurs died during the Flood, while some made it inside the Ark.

After the Flood of Noah, they lived alongside humans and finally went extinct.

> Bring a pair of every kind of animal — a male and a female — into the boat with you to keep them alive during the flood.
>
> — Genesis 6:19

7. We are made according to His image: male and female, for specific purposes.

> So God created human beings in his own image.
> In the image of God he created them;
> male and female he created them.
>
> — Genesis 1:27

 **Our ultimate purpose on Earth is to give glory to God—to tell and show others about Him.**

> *So whether you eat or drink, or whatever you do,*
> *do it all for the glory of God.*
>
> — 1 Corinthians 10:31

 **I am unique. I am God's special Masterpiece.**

> *I praise You because I am fearfully and wonderfully made…*
>
> — Psalm 139:14 NIV

 **I am special in God's eyes. He even knows the number of hairs on my head.**

> *He counts the stars and calls them all by name.*
>
> — Psalm 147:4

For family:

In this busy world today, take time with your family to gaze upon His beautiful creation and point out God's purpose in His amazing works. Remind each other that we are unique creations and we are always in His mind.

For parents:

Parents, create meaningful moments with your children, God's very own masterpieces. They too belong to Him! The Scripture reminds us the time to train our children is now. Don't delay and wait until they are a bit older. "Start children off on the way they should go, and even when they are old they will not turn from it"—Proverbs 22:6 NIV.

Notes

All websites were last accessed on 1/6/2021.

1-1: Theory Buster: The Big Bang

1. "The Universe," European Space Agency, August 20, 2013, www.esa.int/kids/en/learn/Our_Universe/Story_of_the_Universe/The_Universe.
2. "What is the Big Bang?" NASA Science Space Place, June 27, 2019, spaceplace.nasa.gov/big-bang/en/.
3. William Lane Craig, *The Kalām Cosmological Argument* (London: Macmillan Press, 1979).
4. William Lane Craig and Quentin Smith, *Theism, Atheism, and Big Bang Cosmology* (New York: Oxford University Press, 1993), chap. 7 and 8, doi:10.1093/acprof:oso/9780198263838.001.0001.
5. William Lane Craig and James D. Sinclair, "The Kalam Cosmological Argument," *The Blackwell Companion to Natural Theology* (Hoboken, NJ: Wiley-Blackwell, 2009), 101–201, commonsenseatheism.com/wp-content/uploads/2009/05/craig-and-sinclair-the-kalam-cosmological-argument.pdf. This contains an exhaustive bibliography on the Kalam cosmological argument.

1-2: Theory Buster: The Random Chance

1. Michael D. Lemonick, "Q&A: The 5 Ingredients Needed for Life Beyond Earth," National Geographic, June 26, 2014, www.nationalgeographic.com/news/2014/6/140625-kepler-exoplanets-life-astrobiology-goldilocks-nasa/#close.
2. Robin Collins, "The Case for Cosmic Design," Internet Infidels, Inc., 2008, infidels.org/library/modern/robin_collins/design.html.
3. Hugh Ross, "Part 1: Fine-Tuning for Life in the Universe," *Why the Universe Is the Way It Is*, Reasons to Believe (Covina, CA: Reasons to Believe, 2008), d4bge0zxg5qba.cloudfront.net/files/compendium/compendium_part1.pdf.
4. Jerry Coffey, "How Strong is Jupiter's Gravity?" *Universe Today*, June 17, 2008, www.universetoday.com/15110/gravity-of-jupiter/.
5. Richard Pogge, "Lecture 46: Are We Alone? Life in the Universe," The Ohio State University (Astronomy 161 course), November 28, 2007, astro.osu.edu/~pogge/Ast161/Unit7/life.html.

1-3: Theory Buster: Evolution

1. "Biodiversity," National Geographic, August 23, 2019, www.nationalgeographic.org/encyclopedia/biodiversity/. Scientists estimate there are around 8.7 million types of plants and animals living on planet Earth. Only about 1.2 million have been identified so far. Most of them are insects.

2. Charles Darwin, *On the Origin of Species by Means of Natural Selection, or the Preservation of Favoured Races in the Struggle for Life* (London: John Murray, 1859), chap. 14, p. 484, 490, graphics8.nytimes.com/packages/images/nytint/docs/charles-darwin-on-the-origin-of-species/original.pdf.

    "I believe that animals have descended from at most only four or five progenitors, and plants from an equal or lesser number. Analogy would lead me one step further, namely, to the belief that all animals and plants have descended from some one prototype. But analogy might be a deceitful guide….Therefore I should infer from analogy that probably all the organic beings which have ever lived on this earth have descended from some one primordial form, into which life was first breathed."

3. Douglas L. Theobald, "A Formal Test of the Theory of Universal Common Ancestry," *Nature*, 465 (May 2010): 219-222, www.nature.com/articles/nature09014.

4. Bob Strauss, "10 Steps of Animal Evolution from Fish to Primates," ThoughtCo, January 31, 2020, www.thoughtco.com/evolution-of-vertebrate-animals-4040937.

5. Steve and Ruth Carter, "I Really, Really, Really Want to Learn About Ape-Men," Answers in Genesis, June 23, 1997, answersingenesis.org/kids/answers/online-books/really-really-really-learn-about-apemen/.

1-4: Theory Buster: We're Relatives with Chimps!

1. Robert H. Waterson, Eric S. Lander, and Richard K. Wilson, "Initial Sequence of the Chimpanzee Genome and Comparison with the Human Genome," *Nature*, 437 (September 2005): 69–87, www.nature.com/articles/nature04072.

2. Richard Buggs, "How Similar are Human and Chimpanzee Genomes?" July 14, 2018, richardbuggs.com/2018/07/14/how-similar-are-human-and-chimpanzee-genomes/.

3. Jeffrey P. Tomkins, "Comparison of 18,000 De Novo Assembled Chimpanzee Contigs to the Human Genome Yields Average BLASTN Alignment Identities of 84%," *Answers Research Journal*, 11 (September 2018): 205-209, answersingenesis.org/arj/v11/chimpanzee_contig.pdf.

4. Bill Gates, *The Road Ahead* (London: Penguin, 1996), 228.

5. John C. Sanford, *Genetic Entropy* (Waterloo, NY: FMS Publications, 2014).

Notes

1-5: Dinosaurs and Dragons

1. Tia Ghose, "Mesozoic era: Age of the Dinosaurs," Live Science, January 8, 2015, www.livescience.com/38596-mesozoic-era.html. (Below is the first paragraph of Ms. Ghose's article.)

    "During the Mesozoic, or 'Middle Life' era, life diversified rapidly, and giant reptiles, dinosaurs, and other monstrous beasts roamed the Earth. The period, which spans from about 252 million years ago to about 66 million years ago, was also known as the age of reptiles or the age of dinosaurs."

2. Ewen Callaway, "Oldest Homo sapiens Fossil Claim Rewrites Our Species' History," *Nature*, June 2017, www.nature.com/news/oldest-homo-sapiens-fossil-claim-rewrites-our-species-history-1.22114. (Below is a quote from the article.)

    "Researchers say that they have found the oldest Homo sapiens (modern humans) remains on record in an improbable place: Morocco … dated to about 315,000 years ago."

3. Mihai Andrei, "The Age of the Earth – How Do We Know It?" ZME Science, April 25, 2019, www.zmescience.com/science/geology/age-of-the-earth/.

4. "H3117 - yôm - Strong's Hebrew Lexicon (KJV)," Blue Letter Bible, www.blueletterbible.org/lexicon/h3117/kjv/wlc/0-1/.

5. "Dinosaurs and the Bible with Bryan Osborne," *Answers in Genesis* (YouTube channel), streamed live on July 11, 2018, www.youtube.com/watch?v=Y80wHFoYrrQ&t=1603s.

6. Ken Ham, "Dinosaurs and the Bible," Answers in Genesis, November 5, 1999, answersingenesis.org/dinosaurs/dinosaurs-and-the-bible/.

7. Howard Markel and Johanna Mayer, "The Origin of the Word 'Dinosaur,'" Science Friday, July 6, 2015, www.sciencefriday.com/articles/the-origin-of-the-word-dinosaur/.

    The word dinosaur literally means "terrible, powerful, wondrous lizards." The word became popular after a British biologist and paleontologist, Sir Richard Owen, coined the term "Dinosauria" in 1841. The word dinosaur was derived from two Greek words: δεινῖΟἐς (deinós), which means "terrible, powerful, wondrous" and σαά¿¦ρος (saûros) for "lizard."

8. "H8577 - tannîn - Strong's Hebrew Lexicon (KJV)," Blue Letter Bible, www.blueletterbible.org//lang/lexicon/lexicon.cfm?Strongs=H8577&t=KJV.

9. "Inside the Bones," Nova, ScienceNOW, July 2007, www.pbs.org/wgbh/nova/sciencenow/3411/01-insi-nf.html.

    This website lists findings of blood vessels inside the bones of animal fossils that are claimed to be millions of years old.

10. Timothy P. Cleland et al., "Mass Spectrometry and Antibody-Based Characterization of Blood Vessels from *Brachylophosaurus canadensis*," *Journal of Proteome Research*, 14 (November 2015): 5252–5262, pubs.acs.org/doi/pdf/10.1021/acs.jproteome.5b00675.

11. Mary Higby Schweitzer, Jennifer L Wittmeyer, and John R Horner, "Soft Tissue and Cellular Preservation in Vertebrate Skeletal Elements From the Cretaceous to the Present," *Proceedings of Royal Society B*, 274 (January 2007): 183–197, doi.org/10.1098/rspb.2006.3705.

12. Mary H. Schweitzer et al., "Soft-Tissue Vessels and Cellular Preservation in Tyrannosaurus rex," *Science*, 307 (March 2005): 1952–1955, www.sciencemag.org/cgi/content/abstract/307/5717/1952.
13. "The Fascinating Story Behind Dinosaur Soft Tissue," Is Genesis History?, isgenesishistory.com/dinosaur-soft-tissue/.
14. Bodie Hodge, "How Old Is the Earth?" Answers in Genesis, May 30, 2007, answersingenesis.org/age-of-the-earth/how-old-is-the-earth/.
15. André Parrot, "Abraham," Britannica, July 20, 1998, www.britannica.com/biography/Abraham#ref108.

1-6: Where Did All the Dinosaurs Go?

1. Brian Thomas, "Did Dinosaurs Gas Themselves to Extinction?" Institute for Creation Research, June 4, 2012, www.icr.org/article/did-dinosaurs-gas-themselves-extinction/.
2. Bodie Hodge and Georgia Purdom, "What are 'Kinds' in Genesis?" Answers in Genesis, April 16, 2013, answersingenesis.org/creation-science/baraminology/what-are-kinds-in-genesis/.
3. "Noah's Ark and the Flood with Dr. Georgia Purdom," *Answers in Genesis* (YouTube channel), streamed live on July 2, 2018, www.youtube.com/watch?v=6Ma-LP0UDtw&t=1788s.

    Dr. Georgia Purdom presented there were sixty to eighty dinosaur kinds. For more explanation about dinosaur "kinds," check out the explanation in "Were Dinosaurs on Noah's Ark?" Answers in Genesis, July 26, 2020, answersingenesis.org/noahs-ark/were-dinosaurs-on-noahs-ark/.
4. Timothy L. Clarey and Jeffrey P. Tomkins, "Determining Average Dinosaur Size Using the Most Recent Comprehensive Body Mass Data Set," *Answers Research Journal*, 8 (February 2015): 85–91, answersresearchjournal.org/determining-dinosaur-body-mass/.
5. John Woodmorappe, "How Could Noah Fit the Animals on the Ark and Care for Them?" Answers in Genesis, October 15, 2013, answersingenesis.org/noahs-ark/how-could-noah-fit-the-animals-on-the-ark-and-care-for-them/.
6. Walter J. Veith, "Order in the Fossil Record," Amazing Discoveries, February 11, 2009, amazingdiscoveries.org/C-deception-fossils_Paleozoic_Mesozoic_Cenozoic_Flood.
7. Ken Ham, "Dinosaurs and the Bible," Answers in Genesis, November 5, 1999, answersingenesis.org/dinosaurs/dinosaurs-and-the-bible/.
8. "Ice Age," Answers in Genesis, answersingenesis.org/environmental-science/ice-age/.
9. "Dinosaurs and the Bible with Bryan Osborne," *Answers in Genesis* (YouTube channel), streamed live on July 11, 2018, www.youtube.com/watch?v=Y80wHFoYrrQ&t=1603s.

    The second half of the video explains about dinosaurs during and after Noah's flood.

Notes

1-7: God Made Boys and Girls

1. Sue Bohlin, "The Gender Spectrum," Probe Ministries, January 7, 2011, probe.org/the-gender-spectrum/. As opposed to the idea of gender fluidity, introduce the femininity and masculinity gender spectrum to children. The key is to support and encourage different kinds of femininity or masculinity in our children. When they are comfortable in their own skin, they can embrace God's design and grow to be who God made them.
2. Sue Bohlin, "Raising Gender Healthy Kids," Probe Ministries, July 30, 2015, probe.org/raising-gender-healthy-kids/. This article provides some ideas on how to raise gender-healthy children.
3. There are some rare cases of intersexuality, which often involve a chromosomal abnormality. When someone is born with reproductive or sexual anatomy that is not clearly male or female, blood tests generally can reveal if the baby is biologically male or female. In some extremely rare situations, no clear sex is evident. But these rare and complex cases should not be used to change the truth about gender identity.

1-9: God's Unique Masterpiece

1. "Interactive Prenatal Development Timeline," The Endowment for Human Development, www.ehd.org/science_main.php?level=i.
2. Susan J. Lee et al., "Fetal Pain: A Systematic Multidisciplinary Review of the Evidence," *JAMA*, 294 (2005): 947-954, jamanetwork.com/journals/jama/fullarticle/201429#.

   This report concluded: "Evidence regarding the capacity for fetal pain is limited but indicates that fetal perception of pain is unlikely before the third trimester." The third trimester begins at twenty-seven to twenty-eight weeks from conception. They also cited studies using electroencephalography showing that the capacity for functional pain in preterm newborns "probably does not exist before twenty-nine or thirty weeks."
3. Dave Levitan, "Does a Fetus Feel Pain at 20 Weeks?" FactCheck, May 18, 2015, www.factcheck.org/2015/05/does-a-fetus-feel-pain-at-20-weeks/.

   Published research generally supports an experience of pain is possible only later in gestation than twenty weeks. But there are numerous citations on neuroanatomy, development, and related topics; one of these is available at the following site, which endorses the idea pain is experienced at twenty weeks after fertilization: "Fetal Pain: The Evidence," Doctors on Fetal Pain, February 2013, www.doctorsonfetalpain.com/wp-content/uploads/2013/02/Fetal-Pain-The-Evidence-Feb-2013.pdf.
4. Robert Roy Britt, "Lasting Impression: How Fingerprints are Created," Live Science, November 02, 2004, www.livescience.com/30-lasting-impression-fingerprints-created.html.
5. Kate Marple, "Fetal development week by week," BabyCenter, May 22, 2019, www.babycenter.com/pregnancy/your-baby/fetal-development-week-by-week_10406730.

6. Maureen Condic, "When Does Human Life Begin? A Scientific Perspective," *Westchester Institute White Paper Series*, 1 (October 2008), bdfund.org/wp-content/uploads/2016/05/wi_whitepaper_life_print.pdf.

7. "Life in the Womb," Pro-Life Action League, prolifeaction.org/fact_type/life-in-the-womb/.

8. Jess Ford, "Is the Bible Really Pro-Life?" Focus on the Family, September 17, 2020, www.focusonthefamily.com/pro-life/is-the-bible-really-pro-life/.

   Referring to the story of Elizabeth and her unborn baby in Luke 1:39–45, the author wrote: "In conclusion, the Gospels give us a glimpse of the power of Jesus in the womb. It is undeniable that preborn Jesus Christ held immense value. He also carried recognizable individuality, despite Mary only being a few weeks along in her pregnancy….According to the Bible, life is more than just potential, and it is valuable from the moment of conception. Additionally, there is no valid argument for abortion in the Biblical text."

9. Carrie Gordon Earll, "What the Bible Says about the Beginning of Life," Focus on the Family, October 22, 2014, www.focusonthefamily.com/pro-life/what-the-bible-says-about-the-beginning-of-life/.

   "The Bible is far from silent on the topic of the sanctity of human life, especially preborn life in the womb. This resource provides just a few of the Scripture verses that speak to the value of preborn life created in God's image from the moment of fertilization."

10. Scott Klusendorf, "How to Defend Your Pro-Life Views in 5 Minutes or Less," Life Training Institute, prolifetraining.com/wp-content/uploads/2018/09/FiveMinute1.pdf.

    "Suppose that you have just five minutes to graciously defend your pro-life beliefs with friends or classmates. Can you do it with rational arguments? What should you say? And how can you simplify the abortion issue for those who think it's hopelessly complex?"

11. Larry Christenson, *The Wonderful Way Babies Are Made* (Bloomington, MN: Bethany House Publishers, 2000).

1-10: You Are Chosen!

1. "How many stars are there in the Universe?" The European Space Agency, www.esa.int/Science_Exploration/Space_Science/Herschel/How_many_stars_are_there_in_the_Universe.

2. "Current World Population," Worldometers, www.worldometers.info/world-population/.

3. Ken Nelson, "Astronomy for Kids Constellations," Ducksters, www.ducksters.com/science/physics/constellations.php.

PHOTO CREDITS

Welcome to Bible Comes to Life!
Daria Obymaha / Pexels

1-1: Theory Buster: The Big Bang
Tima Miroshnichenko / Pexels
Karolina Grabowska / Pexels
Rakicevic Nenad / Pexels
Neale LaSalle / Pexels

1-2: Theory Buster: The Random Chance
Markus_272 / Shutterstock.com
Pok Rie / Pexels
Pixabay/Pexels
Ben White / Unsplash

1-3: Theory Buster: Evolution
Narikan / Shutterstock.com
Daria Shevtsova / Pexels
LDarin / Shutterstock.com
Pixabay / Pexels
Jill Wellington / Pexels
Aarón Blanco Tejedor / Unsplash

1-4: Theory Buster: We're Relatives with Chimps!
marijn vandevoord / Unsplash
CherylRamalho / Shutterstock.com
BigMouse / Shutterstock.com
Ramona Kaulitzki / Shutterstock.com
David Carillet / Shutterstock.com
Elena Sherengovskaya / Shutterstock.com

1-5: Dinosaurs and Dragons
Fausto García-Menéndez / Unsplash
CHAINFOTO24 / Shutterstock.com
iurii / Shutterstock.com
Christophe BOISSON / Shutterstock.com
Stephen Leonardi / Unsplash

1-6: Where Did All the Dinosaurs Go?
Jon Butterworth / Unsplash
David Clode / Unsplash
Greg Reese / Pixabay
Markus Spiske / Unsplash
Layerace / Freepik.com

1-7: God Made Boys and Girls
Amina Filkins / Pexels
Sergey Mironov / Shutterstock.com
Studio Romantic / Shutterstock.com
miko2 / Shutterstock.com
Olena Yakobchuk / Shutterstock.com
Monkey Business Images / Shutterstock.com
Ahturner / Shutterstock.com
Anna Tamila / Shutterstock.com
Jared Erondu / Unsplash

1-8: Living on Purpose
malith d karunarathne / Unsplash
G-Stock Studio / Shutterstock.com
Andrew Makedonski / Shutterstock.com
SpeedKingz / Shutterstock.com
Priscilla Du Preez / Unsplash

1-9: God's Unique Masterpiece
Katie E / Pexels
Stock Rocket / Shutterstock.com
SciePro / Shutterstock.com
Jianxiang Wu / Unsplash
Everilda / Shutterstock.com
Melica / Shutterstock.com
Aaron Burden / Unsplash
Christopher Cintron / Pexels
RODNAE Productions / Pexels

1-10: You Are Chosen!
Neale LaSalle / Pexels
Valentina Kalashnikova / Shutterstock.com
Aleksandr Ozerov / Shutterstock.com
Paolo Sartorio / Shutterstock.com
Alina Demidenko / Shutterstock.com
Monstera / Pexels
Kamal 2303 / Shutterstock.com

Truth Blast!
Rachel Claire/Pexels

Pages 4–5 and all Activities
Joy Sukadi

About the Authors

Joy Sukadi is a wife, mom of three, and a passionate preacher of God's Word. She has mentored and taught Jesus to women in her community in the past twenty years. She is currently pursuing a Theology Degree at Portland Bible School. Joy also runs a photography business and sees this as an opportunity to connect with local moms. In her spare time, she loves to bike with her family, hike the beautiful Pacific Northwest, do arts and crafts, and play games with her kids. She can't live without Jesus, coffee, and a series of good books.

Lilyana Margaretha is a wife and mom of two girls. She is passionate about equipping Christian parents on how to raise their kids with a biblical worldview. She has a doctoral degree in Molecular and Cellular Biology from the University of Washington. She has a vision of connecting science and the Bible, making it logical, relevant, and applicable in children's lives. Lilyana loves to make crafts, do science with her kids, and enjoy the beauty of the Pacific Northwest with her family.

www.ingramcontent.com/pod-product-compliance
Lightning Source LLC
Chambersburg PA
CBHW042035100526
44587CB00030B/4432